Raecine Tyes

Success Looks Good On Me!

A Soulful Collection of Motivational Excerpts & Spoken Word

2   *Raecine Tyes*

Dedications

To my mom, Lorraine, with love —thanks for always being there for me no matter when, what, where or how...I love you.

To my wonderful husband J. V. — you're my partner, best friend, my lover.
I love you sooo much.

For
Rianni & Dorian — we did it!
Mommy loves you…

Motivation

Raecine Tyes

Motivation

Raecine Tyes

Inspiration (Poems)

Raecine Tyes

Inspiration (Poems)

Raecine Tyes

Acknowledgments

A special thanks to my uncle, Willie Huguley- words can't express my gratitude for your support; it will never be forgotten.

For booking info and additional copies of
Success Looks Good on Me
please contact:
jraemedia@gmail.com

raecine.com

Order your Success Gear t-shirts today!
Wholesale & Retail

Foreword

Don't get it *twisted*! "Success Looks Good on Me" is not your average, run of the mill, "how to" success book. You won't find the usual hum drum, monotone speech in this book that usually accompanies other books on the topic. If you see a word in italics, it's probably because I've used that little twang in my voice for added expression. It's that feeling that I've tried to express to my listener about how passionate I am for their success.

While writing this book I've been known to shout, clap, shake my head or moan as if I were in church. That is the motivating energy I've captured while writing and hopefully the positive emotion I've conveyed throughout each chapter. If you're reading a line and you say to yourself, "I wonder if she's saying that with a little soul in her tone," then you are exactly right. I've dubbed 'Success Looks Good on Me' as "A Soulful collection of spoken word pieces and motivational excerpts."

I've designed the book so you can skip around to whatever captures your attention at the time. Maybe you need a little pick me up because you've dealt with someone who has a less than friendly vibe and you've felt the effects of it. Check out my chapter, "Surround Yourself with Positive People." Perhaps you've involved yourself with a project and have experienced some setbacks, "Disappointments are Steps on the Ladder to Success," is just for you. Or do you have wonderful children who sometimes drive you crazy? You're not the only one! My chapter, "Children are a Blessing" testifies to that.

'Success Looks Good on Me' is a guide to help you draw up the blueprints to *your* success. In this book I've urged you to take the first steps toward creating a vision for yourself and I've encouraged you to achieve it. I've outlined realistic steps that empower you for the purpose of accomplishing your goals. I've given you real life examples to help you see how simple techniques can be self empowering.

It's imperative that you realize *you* are the only person responsible for your own success regardless of any book you've read or workshop you've attended. It's up to you to work the techniques and figure out what's best for you. However, you've started reading my book, so in essence you've taken my hand and allowed me to be a part of your journey. I'm thankful for that. Together we will be focused, determined, and limitless while striving to reach *our* full potential. We'll raise both our hands and say, "Success Looks Good on *Us!*"

All I Ask

For those that don't understand me,
Laugh with me

For those that feel my pain and empathize,
Cry with me

For those that have wisdom and knowledge of self,
Share with me

For those who aren't sure what to do,
Pray for me.

Raecine Tyes

Now or Never!

It's now or never! It's my time to shine! It's my turn!! I've sat back and listened for far too long of other people's philosophy on life, opinions, and their ideas about what they think would or would not work, and why. Of course there were people whose advice I'd cherish, however; I'd been quiet and humble when given unwanted suggestions from people who had no clue on what my vision for my life was. I've seen other people make it to the top of their chosen profession and wonder to myself, "Why haven't I reached that top rung on the ladder yet?" But not anymore-It's my turn! I'd dipped my foot in the pool to see how the water felt, but I'd never made a splash!

In this book, I've recorded my thoughts and experiences in a way that, at least I think are insightful yet humorous. Although, what more can you do but laugh at yourself anyway? Life can't be taken so serious that you miss all the joy in each moment. Before you know it, all of your "every day" moments are going to be cherished memories of the past. You can't sit on the sideline waiting for someone to notice you! First round draft picks aren't labeled such because they sit on the bench, they don't! You have to be out, open and aware of what's going on in your life so that you can successfully be a part of it. I'd sat on my bottom way too long, watching the world go by and not claiming my place in history. We all have natural abilities, God given talents, and I'm sure mine has something to do with interacting positively with people. It's my passion.

 I've always had my thoughts on life, people and the ways we can live the vision that we create for ourselves. I know it's possible to stay motivated and enjoy a fulfilling life, all while inspiring others. The best feeling in the world is to watch a garden grow that you know you've had a hand in getting started, even when all you've done is planted the seeds. It is hoped that by writing this book I've planted some seeds with individuals who desire to live a better quality of life and reach their full potential. In addition to feeling great about accomplishing personal goals, it's always a joy to see another person blossom because of encouragement, inspiration and motivation you've given them. Therefore, my mission is to inspire anyone I can to begin to live the vision they see for themselves. If you begin a project as a result of reading my book, that's good. If you stop a course of life that is nonproductive because of something you've read in my book that is wonderful! If you feel empowered and recognize the greatness that you have within you, that is awesome!

Who is this book for? It is for anyone who wants to be encouraged, empowered, motivated or inspired. Think of this book as a collection of letters written especially for you! The theme of this book is motivational; however, some topics are insight on who I am and why I think the way I do. You'll also have an insider's look at the ideas behind some of my poems. If you read something that doesn't apply to you, do as my grandma use to say and "Just keep on living." In other words, it may not apply to you now, but you never know what your future holds.

Not only is it *my* turn, it's *your* turn as well. It's time to stop feeding into the excuses you've given yourself for so long as to why you're not doing or becoming more in your life. Let go of all the reasons you have for not accomplishing goals you've set in the past. Weren't you supposed to take a class or start school? Are you afraid to change careers but instead you continued to stay at a job you hated? Wasn't it a couple of years ago that you promised yourself to drop a few pounds? Wasn't it you who said you weren't going to put up with that 'thing' this year that you endured last year? Start right now and take the first step of reclaiming the 'You' that you'd like to become. Get a pencil and some paper and write down all the goals you set for yourself, whether large or small. Next, check off the goals that you've actually completed. For the ones that don't have a check, write another list. This time jot down all the *lame* excuses you produced as to why you haven't completed a project or vision for yourself. My 'excuses' list consisted of nearly the *same* excuses, in each circumstance; Scenarios that could have been worked around and in some cases avoided all together.

Now, if you happen to be one of the people that had most of your goals checked off, which means you completed them, that's great! So, instead of creating a list of excuses, you can come up with some ideas on how you can immediately improve on being you. I know, I know, there is the old saying 'If it ain't broke, don't fix it.' Yes and I understand that, but you can certainly make some improvements. I'm positive that every person can, no matter *who* you are. I know that whoever invented the wheel would definitely be in awe at the improvements made to that basic invention. Imagine riding down the expressway with a wooden wheel and no shocks! Ouch! That picture alone makes you appreciate 'improvements' that much more.

Improving on yourself doesn't mean you have to change who you are. Build on the positive qualities that you already possess. This is something everyone can do, whether you've already made achievements in your lifetime or not. If you haven't created goals for yourself then start thinking of some realistic ways to become a better you!

Write Right Now

I'll be scribbling to my last breath
Writing words until there's none left
I've used all letters in the alphabet and then some
I'm taking advice from an old movie "write and they will come"

I used to write from dusk to dawn,
Now I go from sun to sun
I used to write for business
Now I write for fun

I used to keep quiet, but that's in the past
Time don't stop for no one, so I'm writing fast
I'm not going to let any opportunity pass

I'll even stop ya', and read to you if I see ya'
Maybe I'll hook up with Tyler and write a play about Madea
"I'm so analytical about my write –TING,
To see my words in print is so excite-TING"

I'm like Carl when I write, so emotional,
I get caught up
I'm hoping the shelves, in the store, with my books, will be empty
All bought up

After you read I'll even ask you, "Its real good, isn't it?"
Like when I'm cookin', I'll give you my best,
I put my foot in it

I'm so, so, so,
Just like Floetry
I call what I do writing words
I'm not sure if I consider it Poetry
You never knew me before
But now you know of me

I'm a beast and the whites of my teeth are showing
The more that I write, the more my repertoire is growing

Raecine Tyes

I went to the doctor worried I was becoming fanatical
He said take two weeks off and write some more
A writing sabbatical

My words are motivational, nothing fancy
But if I don't have pen and paper in hand,
I'll start to get antsy

Everything that I do is so entrepreneurial
To help you get started, I'll even write a tutorial

Every word that I choose I use with careful decision
My pen to the paper is a scalpel I call it writing precision
Because when you understand me,
You understand my vision

Writing is my passion and I plan on exploiting every bit of it
 It's an obsession I have; I'll gratify it until I'm rid of it

I'm delivering my writing pieces
Faster than Papa John delivers its pizzas
My writing is so good you'll try to eat it
If writing was a sport, I'd be undefeated

I take my writing serious; it's no longer a game to me
Ain't nothing left but fame for me
I'm dying to prove myself and show off my abilities
I got two kids to feed, by any means

Writing Fanatic

I'm a writing fanatic
It used to be a private obsession
But now it's a daily habit

For years I stopped
But I'm back at it
Just like an addict

Constantly,

I'm feigning for a pen to scribble down a thought
Cost of my pen- two dollars
Cost of my words - priceless
They can never be bought

I'm in a writing frenzy
I'm every author's envy
Like Mary Mary
It's the writing *in* me

My writing appeals to all
It's non-denominal
Sometimes I sit back and read what I write
And say to myself- Phenomenal

Look Ma, I'm Writing!

My one main hurdle in starting this book was to pinpoint a topic that I could write passionately about, subject matter slightly controversial yet provocative enough to catch a person's attention. After sharing some of my ideas with my brother, his suggestion was to write about interracial relationships. "Why do Black men date White women?" he asked. "Now *that* would be controversial, *and* you can get a lot of people involved," he added. "Naaah," I thought, and probably said aloud. That is a topic people have all but worn out. Anyway that doesn't excite me, I'm not in an interracial relationship, and never have been. He, on the other hand, well, maybe my next book should be about him.

While rushing to the bank to deposit $20 into my checking account, so that it won't overdraw, it hit me! There has got to be someone who wants to hear the struggle of a single, black mother on her way to the top; a woman who is so confident in her own success that she allows you to tag along on her journey. Writing this book is an aspiration that I've contemplated time, after time, after time. However, in the past I always allowed malleable circumstances to dictate who I was and the direction I was going instead of me taking control and doing what I really loved. The sad part is I accepted the excuses and deemed them sufficient for not becoming more successful and not aspiring to do more in my life.

Now, I'm choosing to set my life standards at a higher level than I normally aim for and surprisingly, I'm forgoing the usual sabotage of my own success. I am so good at the self-sabotaging that I have it down pat. It has become a bore at this stage in my life, so much so that I've decided to take a different route and go in the other direction. I vow here and now to make some life changing accomplishments, which means I will have to follow through regardless of any obstacles. What could be more tantalizing than that?

Entertainers, top executives, entrepreneurs and gurus sometimes speak of the path they took to success maybe 10 or 20 years earlier in their lives, but more than a few have summed up the years they had struggling, if any, into a mere one or two sentences. "Yes, I once lived in a one bedroom apartment, but I made it out with the help of… '*My System*'" says a deep, velvety, polished voice of a narrator whose main objective is to get the viewer to purchase a product or program. The remainder of the time they speak of big contracts or risky investments they made that ultimately propelled them to the status they now attain. What "everyday" person can relate to that? Really, who else will fess up to depositing a lousy $20 into a bank account?

My goal isn't to give you the golden secret to success, although I do have an opinion on that. What I want to do however is share insight on my world and maybe open some minds to ponder, as I have, about the little things in life that make us who we are. I'd like for anyone reading this book to think about a topic in a fresh new light that he or she hadn't considered before. And maybe, just reading this will give someone inspiration to start or complete a life changing project of his or her own. It's my desire that a person read about frivolous decisions I made and learn from them. In fact, I want you to look at what I went through and say, "You know that Raecine, she made some dumb mistakes. I know now not to do that." And if you've experienced similar situations, know that you aren't alone. Just as I heard someone say today, "Just because you fall down, doesn't mean you have to stay down. Pick yourself up and keep going." I figure, if this book inspires at least one person to *do something*, then I can claim 'mission accomplished'.

 I know that I've gotten inspired to start projects from the oddest of motivators. For example, so many times I'd find myself talking back to the television, wondering why a seasoned journalist has not asked a particular question of her guest or not highlighted other pertinent ideas that would shed more light on the subject matter. Also, more than once I voluntarily have offered my synopsis on how a movie will or should end, and when correct in my assumption, I playfully force praise from my children by overly enthusiastically declaring, "I told you that would happen! Didn't I?? I *told* you! I knew it! I can write this stuff." Their nonchalant replies, "Yup mommy, you did," led me to believe it was time to convince someone who actually cared.

However, as a spoken word artist, I know that I can only get started writing and complete a book only if my words sound right, flow right, and have a satisfying rhythm. I don't want to sound like other authors whose books I pick up at a Barnes and Noble and immediately put down after reading a couple of paragraphs, believing that a visit with my dentist would be easier to endure. I also don't want to seem as if I am searching for words and then making them stay on the page against their will. I promised myself to begin writing only if the words flowed to my mind easily and comfortably. That they have; as I sometimes find myself racing to find a pen and paper or personal recorder to catch a passing thought. I always knew that if I opened my mind to the possibility of being an author, I'd succeed.

So here I am. It's my turn to vent my thoughts, opinions, observations, fears, elations, aspirations, accomplishments and even inadequacies; I'm risking it all, and putting it on paper for anyone interested. This has got to be the best therapy in the world, and I'm assuming considerably cheaper than an average session. My only hope is that as a novice writer, my thoughts and words evoke the same passion and emotion in the reader that I had while writing them.

What is your passion? Maybe you have the skills to do something that you love, but feel you don't have the time to pursue it. Do you involve yourself with what you love to do on a daily basis? Can you incorporate your passion into your career? Have people told you that you're so good at something that you need to be in business for it? If your talents are recognizable to your family and friends, maybe you have a gift that should be developed. *If you have opportunities to share your gift with others, take it!* A person is usually good at whatever it is they desire to do.

The desire you have in your heart for your passion, is undeveloped talent waiting to flourish! Don't deprive the world of the gift God has blessed you with. Tap into your full potential; share your talent with everyone you know. Let the world know what you have to offer and watch new and exciting opportunities open up for you, which align themselves with your passion!

It's My Turn

You wanna come in and steal all my glory?
Make big promises and come up short on me?

I told y'all before this ain't no game to me
If I fall short this time rising to the top,
Blames on me
Shame on me!

What you think you got that I can't get for myself?
All I need in this life is God's glory and good health

Because yeah, just like Black wealth
I may be scarce, but I'm making it happen

Regardless of all circumstances!

You never get em'
So I'm taking all my chances
And making advances
To a life that I choose

I paid my dues!

Twenty years, cutting hair, in a barber chair
Clippers in one hand, baby sittin' right there!

Kicked to the street, while working over 40 hours a week
Professing my love, to what I thought was positive and Black
Turns out, that n----- on crack!

Baby daddy just got out from doing a 13 year bid,
Now, how the hell is that supposed to affect my kid?!

So, don't come telling me something you think I ain't heard before
I been thru some s--- ! And I ain't tryin' to go thru more

And don't get it twisted, I ain't new to the game,

I been playin for years
Difference is, I've erased all doubt and I'm facing my fears

It's my turn

I'm doin' it big
It's my turn to prosper
It's my turn to live

No more second guessing myself
Or missed opportunities
I'm living who I choose to be

I'm placing proper importance on my top priorities
My kids and me

I'm living my life so I can aspire
And rise higher
Towards Gods plan for me

My Legacy

Passionately, I speak

I want to convey a feeling,
That has been building
Inside

A swelling, so overwhelming,
that not telling, could be
detrimental

Fervently, I write

because my mind is getting clouded,
from all the words that are shouting
They each need their own space in time
so, on paper I put them

I am delighted that each of my words is in a friendly competition

With wisdom and time, each set will be at its best
seeking to inspire anyone that stops to listen

Grammatically, my words yearn for each other,
as a family, they form a composition,
they are repetitive when necessary
And determined when faced with opposition

Some of my words I've kept hidden for years
for lack of self confidence and personal fears

But recently, I've been releasing them
Increasingly having faith that they'll unceasingly
speak for themselves,
my story, they promised to tell

I desire to leave a legacy, with many dimensions, not to mention
lessons learned and wisdom

Raecine Tyes

A trail of words as eager to speak, as ears that will listen

A legacy, I wish to leave, with words I decidedly choose
A recognized gift to me, now I'll appropriately use

It's My Turn

My desire to write has finally caught up with me. An avid reader, I usually immerse myself in self-help, motivational and inspirational books. Previous to writing this book, it seemed as if a collection of material I read in the past was hollering out to me in unison, saying, "Do something! Write something! Involve yourself in a project that will show the world your passion!"

Procrastination aside, I decided it was now or never. I will write; I will write to let the universe know that I am here, I am alive, and I do have something to say. My two cents may not amount to much; nonetheless, I want to be heard. Therefore, count me in; I want to play on the team. I may not hit a homerun, but I'm not going to leave the field before I at least give it a try.

When I began writing this book, I felt it was finally time to share my voice with the world; it's my turn to let everyone know what's on my mind. It's my turn to share my experiences and give the life lessons I learned from them. It's my turn to push, encourage and empower anyone who needs it, because we all don't have the luxury of a perfect support system. It's not easy to find someone who believes wholeheartedly in the vision you have for your life, but I'm here to tell you that "I got your back!" Go for whatever it is in the back of your mind that motivates you each day to dream and aspire to become more, because that's exactly what I'm doing right now. I'm finally taking my turn to hopefully inspire someone to greatness, encourage someone to become and do more with his or her life, or at least experience a better quality of life.

So, if while reading my book, I happen to sound a bit preachy, it's only because I'm trying to instill in you the importance of striving to reach your full potential. That's the only way you're going to be at your best. I don't claim to have all the answers in this book and I'm definitely not at the level of success that I believe I am capable of achieving. I always tell people I'm a work in progress, because I'm always trying to accomplish more. Every day I do my best to take my own advice and make it work. Have you ever discussed something with a friend, a subject you already knew about, but for some reason when you talked with them, at that particular time, it finally clicked with you? Your friend was the sounding board you needed. My hope is that this book is encouragement for you to act on knowledge you already possess. We can all use some support at some point, if only to keep us on track and to continue making progress.

After reading my poem, "My Apologies, A Letter to All Haters" one person asked me why was I so angry. I wasn't angry when I wrote that, I was excited! I was excited because I knew that I was no longer settling for mediocrity in my life. I knew it was time to get in high gear because I was about to start experiencing the feeling that accompanies confidence and the successful completion of a lifelong goal.

However, if getting angry is what it takes to get a fire lit under you to create a vision for your life, accelerate your current pace or to improve at any level of success you are enjoying now, then get angry! Get as mad as you have to if it will make you realize how far you could've gotten while either procrastinating or telling yourself you can't do something. Stop listening to negative input and do something about it! You're worth it, you have the ability and it's your right to claim your turn in life to do whatever your passion is, just as I am now.

Vibe Session

Remember when you wrote a few words down on paper?
Expressing your goals and describing your future: "safer"
Well, now its sooner, rather than later
Time to forget all the haters
Elohiem, we god...our own soul's creator
It's time to strive for something greater

Tweet me, with an inspirational thought
Don't tell me the lesson you learned
Show me the lesson you taught
Don't complain about who sold out
Just make sure you don't get bought

Motivate with your words
Consider your life a blessing
Let go and let God

So, no reason for stressin"
I'm confessin'

That the mere effervescence of my presence
won't be lessened

If you take a moment to chill
And step in my Vibe Session

Keep it Movin'

Its quarter past, and Opportunity has passed
Life won't stop and wait for you to "get it together"
Time isn't going to hold out his hands for you

Whatever you have in your head as a vision
You'd better get on with it

No one is going to play out your scenario
You're the only one in this scene
Do you know your lines?
This isn't dress rehearsal

What are you sitting down waiting for?
Public transportation stopped running hours ago
Are you trying to catch a ride, with any passerby?
What if he's not going your way?

What are you going to do when people say:
"I thought you would have arrived by now"
Well, its not about them
You are the only one, slowing you down

Look, the sun's coming up
That's Opportunity rising
Are you going to catch it today?

The only way that you'll be successful
Is if you keep it movin'.

Inspiration

I have read numerous books about success, motivation, and inspiration. The basic principles of becoming successful and staying motivated all require some degree of planning, persistence, and flexibility. These three key items are valuable to anyone's success. You can motivate yourself with pep talks or by keeping busy with constructive activities that lead to your goals.

Inspiration, however, is a little spark that binds everything together. Perhaps you've been working a project for some time, but you feel there is something missing. Along comes a word, a sight or a sound that makes something click within you. Some people describe this as a Eureka moment. A perfect example of this was Walt Disney. He was already motivated and had some measure of success as a cartoonist; however, when a mouse ran past him in his garage, it inspired him to create Mickey Mouse. It is so important to stay active so you won't miss out on your inspirational moments; *Flashes of energy that only last a split second, but so powerful, they can change not only your life, but also others as well.*

Inventors and inventions too, have had that same effect. Most inventions took years to perfect because it wasn't until something inspired the developer to think in a certain way that a final, successful product evolved, and gratefully so. Today many people may take innovation for granted, forgetting that it was more than likely an inspirational moment that caused an inventor's idea to become a reality. Your inspirational moments could mean the difference in your life being mediocre or becoming extraordinary.

If you are reading my book for inspiration, I would be doing you an injustice by not pressing you to *do more and become more active in the pursuit of your goals,* whatever they may be. You must start today in taking steps to accomplish something toward the vision you have for yourself! If you do not have a clear vision of what you want for your life, which includes a plan on how to reach your goals, then that is your first step. A simple list of ideas is a good start. Make an unfiltered list of every passion you have, activities that bring you joy, careers you have considered in the past, or life dreams. Next, jot down what you would have to do to make your ideas become a reality. Is there a class you should enroll in? Do you need to start saving money for a project or would a phone call to gather information on a particular topic help? Anyone one of these paths can be the catalyst that will make the difference in the fruition of your vision. With all factors in place, and you working toward accomplishing your goals, you are creating opportunities for an abundance of inspirational moments in your life.

Just Say Yes!

I've done inside and outside sales, business to business marketing and I've even peddled religious material in residential neighborhoods. I've even sold items in the Wal-Mart parking lot as a street vendor. The one thing that I noticed most people had in common was they would say "no" to what I offered sometimes before they even got a chance to find out what the product was. I'd always wish that for just once I could reply to their "no" with, "Oh! So, you *don't* want the two million dollars that I was going to give to you, just because?" It was almost as if people were programmed to say no. Most times if a person didn't want to be bothered, they'd tell me, "I'm not interested." Well my question is, "What is it that you aren't interested in, because I haven't told you anything yet." And most of the deals I had were pretty good ones. Of course, if those potential customers said yes, it would've benefited the both of us. I would've gotten a commission from the sale and they would've received a great price on whatever I was offering. However, my point is, they wouldn't know of the great deal they were missing out on or have a chance to experience a great new service simply because their minds were closed to the idea from the start.

It's kind of ironic but I've heard so many individuals complain that exciting new things never happen to them. They grumble that they always do the same thing from day to day. They spread vicious talk that certain things are not possible in life because they've never seen or had particular scenarios play out within their own existence. What I've realized though is sometimes you might say no to opportunity without realizing it. You may think that because you haven't said the actual word no to something specific, that it doesn't apply. But think about it. You don't know *when* or *how* a life changing event is going to take place. If you consistently have a closed mind about new ideas, projects, travel, business ventures or meeting new people, than you are in effect saying no to new opportunities. With those simple projects, ventures or ideas, there may come along better experiences. Those lead to even bigger chances of you reaching your goals or getting closer to the vision that you have for yourself.

I was always told as a child that when someone offered me something, even a second hand gift, that I should say yes and accept it. Be appreciative and accept the gift even if what was given was not what you'd ordinarily choose for yourself. First, because the gesture extended to you was thoughtful and secondly, they'd think of you the second time around when that *next* gift might happen to have much more value. Imagine if you refused the first present of hardly any value. Why would they offer you more or anything for that matter, the next time around? I know I wouldn't.

Don't get it twisted though. Saying yes isn't always the answer to everything. Think about the outcome. If you have a negative outlook and a closed mind on any situation, how far will that get you? Have you weighed the pros and cons for your scenario? Will saying yes help you to get closer to reaching your goals? Perhaps you have the potential to gain valuable skills and knowledge because you opened yourself up to a new set of circumstances. Were you asked to volunteer for a non-profit? Have you been invited out by a friend to meet new people? Were you offered a position at work that you weren't familiar with? Did a friend ask a time consuming favor of you? Where you offered a gift of little to no value? What were your answers? Consider saying yes more than you say no, and watch an entire new world of opportunity open up to you.

You Don't Get Chances, You Take Them!

Senior year for the class of 1989, and the halls in my high school were alive and buzzing with the excitement of a fast approaching graduation. Graduate portraits had already been taken and everyone was frantically deciding on what quirky quote to place beneath pictures in the yearbook. I was tired of the exhausted phrases chosen each year to describe individual personalities and life theories. I needed something different, new, and mesmerizing.

I wanted to create a short, simple quote that could motivate or inspire anyone who read it into action. I didn't want to state anything too complex, just a few words that would make a person think. Perhaps after reading my one liner, a reader would nod her head in agreement or even utter the soulful groan of "uh huh" as parishioners do when they hear something that has touched them deep inside. I was resolute not to place a meaningless saying beneath my name for the sheer joy of sounding cute. I thought long and hard each day of a few short words that would not only capture my outlook on life, but also captivate anyone who read it for a possible spark of inspiration.

Suddenly, it came to me. So busy in the pursuit of everyday living, people are always saying that they didn't get a chance to do or complete something. In addition, others list activities and projects or goals that they will aspire to, only after they *get* a chance. Wait a minute! *No one is promised an hour in advance or even the next few minutes of life on this earth.* If you have an idea, project, book, a goal or whatever that it may be that you are striving for or want to complete, your best bet is to get started immediately! This dramatic thinking also aided me in putting an end to my procrastinating habits.

"You don't get chances, you take them," are the words that popped in my head while scribbling crazily trying to come up with something original before the yearbook deadline. Unfortunately, I missed the closing date. The one liner that I worked so hard to create never even appeared publicly for the world to see. Nonetheless, I've lived by that way of thinking ever since that day, taking chances to create opportunities for myself, which otherwise may not have

Raecine Tyes

materialized on their own. When situations occur and friends or family opt out for fear of failure, I choose to play risky, reasoning with myself to take a chance because wonderful possibilities could result.

Spoken Word (Look at Me)

With adrenaline pumping, I first stepped on stage
to engage,
in a light hearted slam session

little did I know it would become an obsession
I became a junkie of sorts, traveling back and forth
Seeking out open mics for my next spoken word lesson

Intently I listened to every word spoken
Careful, not to take for granted,
Keeping my mind open

Desperate to prove my abilities as a poet
I didn't know if
My skills were good enough
So, I put them to the test

I was blessed,
being in the presence of those considered the best

Performing on stage was my symbolic plateau
of the ground I'd have to cover, the distance I'd go

Delivering metaphoric speeches
Avoiding all the words that end with 'ism'
I had to trust in

my poetry to stand alone
and take on a tone, of its own
Spoken word was my calling
so I picked up the phone

Years past and I didn't do spoken word that much
I was afraid I'd lost my touch
It was a tragedy, quite sad for me

Because I still had so many things to express
I digressed, nonetheless

Raecine Tyes

But now I'm back on point
With not only spoken word, but there's other things I dabble in
If you don't stop to listen, you might think I'm babbln'

Now motivation is my number one priority
so in the majority
of my spoken word pieces, people I try to inspire
I've even become a writer

Selected eclectic pieces I've collected from my past
secured them in a memoir, so at last
I'll share my life lessons, my learning was vast,

Although numerous
some were quite humorous

But my ultimate goal is inspiration
to provide encouragement and stimulation

to anyone with low self confidence
I trust in their competence

Success is planning, persistence and flexibility
stay focus on achieving, if it's a vision that you see
be intent on becoming, rather than just be

and if you need a true to life example
take a look at me.

Spoken Word

I started performing spoken word about 12 years ago at the prodding of a good friend. Although we wrote and produced some songs together, he had never heard my poetry previous to convincing me to attend a local open mic. I'm not sure if he didn't want to be the only new performer that night or if he just needed a ride; but he told me early in the afternoon to prepare a piece of poetry and be ready to perform it that same evening. He was confident that I could do it. "Gurrl, you can do this!" he said. All the while I was thinking to myself, "Is he crazy? Me? Poetry?" I was going to give him a ride to the venue regardless, *and* jot something down for the sake of creating a piece, but there was no way in the world I was going to perform.

However, after meeting some fresh faces, hearing other poems and catching the vibe, I did it! With adrenaline rushing through my body, I performed a saucy piece about being in love. To me, it was quite corny, as I was paraphrasing what a young girl in love would think and feel. To my surprise, the audience loved it! They laughed at the funny parts, nodded in agreement when I changed my mood and tone, and seemed to grasp every little point I was trying to convey. They understood me. That was a good feeling. All it took was that one time and I was a spoken word junkie.

For about a year, he and I traveled to all the local poetry slams we could find. At his cajoling, I performed in New York's Nuyorican poetry club. I even produced and promoted some of my own events. Each time I performed, I got the same reaction of acceptance from listeners and other poets.

I never truly felt as if I were a poet though, they all seemed to think so deeply about life and I wasn't sure if I lived up to that. I met so many different types of poets: romantic, political, militant, the one who always spoke about being naked and many more. I had my opinions about current events or relationships that I would inject into my poems, but I didn't fit into any of the cliques.

I always believed that being a poet was a way of life. I had too many other distractions than to engross myself totally with poetry. Being able to get an instant reaction from listeners in the crowd, and afterwards talking one-on-one with the audience, really gave my self confidence a boost though. I liked being able to express myself in my own words and inspire individuals to think about what I was saying. It was then that I realized I didn't want to sing for people, I wanted to speak to them.

Healthy Me

One of the most important things we can do each day to show appreciation for the life God gave us is to individually care for ourselves. Simple checkups with a doctor, exercise or eating properly can all attribute to good health. As a procrastinator, these are things that I had to work at to turn into healthy habits.

Sometimes our acquaintances need a gentle nudge to care for an aspect of their health they may have bypassed. Perhaps it's a wakeup call to stop some unhealthy, perilous habit or a reminder for them to just eat healthier. Maybe it concerns a matter of hygiene. Have you ever thought that it may be you who can successfully direct him or her to what needs attention and perhaps ultimately salvage his or her wellbeing?

Too many times we take good health for granted until something happens to us in a major way. It is hoped that anyone reading this with chronic health conditions has the strength, resources and support from others necessary to manage his or her situation.

It wasn't until age 37 that I stepped back and assessed my own life. Fortunately, I haven't had anything to complain about concerning my health. I was however a few pounds heavier than I would've like to be and a little more stressed than usual. Weight control has never been a big deal for me though. For example, I know that when my bottom starts getting big, its time to stop eating and start walking. This year too, I realized that health clubs only work when you go inside and actually exercise, not just when you register with a membership.

I also found firsthand that too much stress is no laughing matter. Stress can physically damage your body and kill you, if not controlled. Excessive acid in your stomach, a reoccurring headache or chest pain, is sometimes a physical manifestation of something worrying or bothering you. The fastest way I deal with stress is a long, very hot shower. It helps me to instantly relax and refocus my attention on whom and what is most important in my life. Stretching and listening to music are also ways I unwind and let go of tension and stressing thoughts. Cleaning too, allows my mind time to regroup and prioritize; instead of worrying about situations that only time can change.

Taking time out of a hectic schedule to spend quietly with yourself can work wonders for frazzled nerves. Spending recreational time with family is also a good way to renew yourself and build a healthy family relationship.

I have zero tolerance for non-medical, chemical dependency. Substance abuse is something I have never had to deal with personally or within my immediate family; I can't even tolerate cigarette smoke. I can only urge people to consider everything they do to their bodies and think about the long term effects for themselves and those that love them.

Assess your own life as I did mine. Is stress overwhelming you? Are you successfully dealing with stress? No one else is going to care for yourself the way that you can. Always try to keep a good attitude and be optimistic with a positive mind. Negative thoughts are toxic and take a toll on your body with some of the same physical symptoms as stress. I've seen some people take better care of their cars, than their own body! Do everything that you can to keep yourself strong, healthy and happy. Not only do you want to *look* good, make sure what's under *your* hood is running good too.

My Personal Pledge

Naturally intricate, my body
A treasure, respectfully kept

From the oils I smooth on my skin that softens its touch
To spiritual food I place within, so desperately necessary

I regard my body as beautiful, rightfully so
I am a wonderfully made soul

Daily, I bathe myself, and refresh my spirit
Faithfully, I cleanse my mind, with uplifting thoughts

I affectionately brush my hair, attention it garners
Not matter how much, it is glorious

My eyes, from which energy flows, show
that I am well rested

Teeth, adamantly preened,
declare my devotion, to my wellbeing

The healthiest foods I select to nourish me
By keeping fit, I attain vitality

My nails are a reflection of my gratitude,
so, tidily I keep them
Soles of my feet, I have not forgotten
With creams and lotions, I adorn them

Tastefully, I clothe myself
I have a positive aura

My self esteem soars
as I attest to my personal pledge
"Vanity is useless,
so, with humility I gratefully
and graciously care for me"

Raecine Tyes

Donuts, Loosies and Liquor

I know I'll get some haters on this chapter for sure, but I'm sorry. I'm going in on this topic with a vengeance! I'm not a fitness guru, a weight loss counselor or even a nutritionist. But I do know what is good for my body and I recognize the things that are harmful. I also have a few common sense guidelines that I follow regarding what is conducive to good health and what practices aren't. Take a look at your fitness regime, your daily eating habits, and your lifestyle then ask yourself, "Is what I do to my body on a consistent basis contributing to a long, healthy life?"

I'll never forget the day I was standing at a bus stop in D.C. and a young woman and her son came and sat down on the bench next to me. She appeared to be in her twenties and her child was probably about 3 years of age. It was early in the morning, so it wasn't a surprise that she pulled out something to munch on as we waited for the bus. However, what bothered me was what she and her child proceeded to eat: glazed donuts and bacon. I know that of the people reading this, some might chuckle because they figure those food choices are nothing out of the ordinary, and you probably had the same meal today or earlier this week. Therefore you may ask yourself, "What's the big deal?"

On the other hand, there are those people reading this that may be shaking their head, knowing those are the least healthy of foods she could've chosen to feed herself and her son. Did I mention that even though the woman, (who was about half my age) was literally about three times my weight? She was in fact, overweight. She either had no clue of what regularly eating those foods did to her body, or she didn't care. I don't know what the fat content on each food item alone is, but I can only imagine what consuming foods like that everyday can do to you. Your weight, blood and heart are just a few things that take a toll with a diet similar to hers.

 Do yourself a favor and make a log of everything you eat for one week. Write down *everything* that you eat and drink, for seven days. No matter what it is, even if it is a quick snack you got from the vending machine at work; *especially* if it is a quick snack from the vending machine at work. At the end of the week, make a quick review of things like the calorie, fat, sugar and sodium content of everything you've consumed. You may be surprised at what you find. If you don't understand the figures or if you are unsure about what you are reading, ask someone in the health or fitness field the importance of your log. Find out why you should keep those things leveled within your diet. Read about the consequences each has on your body. *Educate yourself on how to take care of yourself.*

I can remember health class in school as a mandatory class that was given for probably one semester, and then entirely forgotten. Good health is something you have to work at every day. I think if more knowledge was given to individuals about the immediate effects of particular foods or substances in their body, they'd make better decisions when it comes to what goes *in* their body. A health conscious person is not necessarily a health nut; he is simply someone who is aware of what is productive or detrimental to his body. No one is going to give you 'good health.' You can't stand in line, as if you're waiting for government cheese, to have it handed to you. You have to get your own! When you purchase your foods, ask yourself, "What is this going to do to my body?"

I'm here to tell you that if you don't know, find out! And if you don't care, then get some wits about you, wake up and start taking care of yourself. Everything that you put in your body has an effect on your well-being (or not so well-being). Realize that what you do to yourself, including your health and your mental status, all play a part on you living up to your full potential. Do yourself a favor. Don't even get started with bad habits that have no positive outcomes, no pros and only cons. I've never smoked a cigarette a day in my life and I've never desired to. If you are a smoker, ask yourself, "Why am I smoking? How did I get started? Why do I continue to smoke even though I know it's harmful to me and others in my presence?" Every smoker that I was personally involved with got very touchy about the subject, although I'd never try to persuade them to quit. I know that was a matter of personal preference and something they'd have to decide, in their own mind and timeframe, to do.

Thinking back, it's funny how one of my past relationships, he tried to convince me that we were soul mates and he wanted to have children with me. One day I thought to myself, "Hmm, he's practically a chain smoker and he drinks a fifth of liquor everyday when he gets home from work. Naaah, I don't envision my soul mate doing those things." I had to realize that his lifestyle practices didn't click with mine and no matter how much love there was, the way he treated his body was something that bothered me. Our baby would've come into the world with a lighter in one hand and a nip in the other!

"That doggone Raecine! I really enjoyed reading her book *until* she started talking about smoking cigarettes and drinking liquor. Who does she think she is anyway? She ain't nobody, she ain't even cute!" If this topic is bothering you, then good! Put those stank cigarettes down! Stop drinking so much! If nobody else is going to tell you, I will. If other friends and family members have mentioned your habit to you, don't get mad at them. If they didn't care, they wouldn't say a thing to you. Perhaps they've stopped bugging you already, because you gave them 'the business' when they did get on your case. Well, don't! And, save your breath. We all know the scripture about the rafter in our own eyes *and* no one is trying to judge you. That isn't the case. And stop giving that sorry one liner about it's your life and how everyone is different and your momma lived and smoked until she was 110 years old. *Whateverrrr*! You're killing yourself!

As regards the alcohol, don't get it twisted! I'm talking about the people who drink as if liquor is kool-aid. You can find them drinking hard liquor solely because they are thirsty. (Yeah, right.) And to those of you who have to have that 'one drink' everyday to calm your nerves, ask yourself, "If I had to, can I stop or am I addicted?"

These are some difficult things to face and think about; people always like to hear how great they are, no matter what they are doing, whether it is positive or negative. They don't want someone telling them what they shouldn't be doing, especially if that messenger is a close friend or family member. Well good, I'm neither.

I'm not bashing you for the lifestyle that you chose for yourself. I'm simply asking you to consider all the choices you make and realize the impact they have on you and the people that love you. Cherish your health and remember that once it's gone, it's gone. You can have all the dreams, goals and intentions in the world. But if you don't have the strength, health or vitality to follow through, then you have nothing. Be real with yourself and ask yourself what changes you can make to live a more fulfilling life. Your life is a gift. Enjoy a healthy presence.

You're Blessed

You're blessed!
But you didn't notice
because you were too busy keeping track of things gone wrong

You were blessed!
But you didn't realize it
because you were complaining that the blessing you requested
was taking too long

You've been blessed!
But you didn't feel the effects
because you were too drunk or too high

You're blessed!
But you don't have a clue
because instead of aspiring for more
you are content with just getting by

Unbeknown to you

You were blessed!
But you didn't know
because you were too busy scheming, trying to get over on someone

You've always been blessed!
But you didn't reap the rewards
because instead of putting in work
you just wanted to have fun

You were blessed!
But you weren't grateful
because you were too busy being hateful
on another person's blessing

You received a blessing!
But you didn't understand that it came in the form of a lesson
So, instead of learning from it
You used it as another vice for stressing

You were blessed!
but your lack of humility
didn't allow you to accept an opportunity
that you thought was beneath you
so, that blessing passed you by

You were blessed!
But you didn't acknowledge that it came from God
instead you praised *yourself*
and you didn't thank Him

You are blessed!

Open your eyes to all your blessings
With God, they are constantly manifesting

Be thankful!

Be grateful!

Be blessed!

Make Yourself Top Priority

If you don't make yourself your own top priority, who else will? No one else can live your dreams or create a vision for your life that you will be passionate about, but you! You are the only person capable of designing a life that you have complete control over. When you don't make yourself top priority, that's when outside influences have control of your circumstances, and you become a victim of your environment. Have you ever been at a gathering with friends and it came time to vote on what to eat? If you didn't speak up and let your friends know what you wanted, you probably ended up eating whatever someone else ordered, like it or not. Never sit quietly and let "the room" speak for you. Speak up and express yourself especially when the outcome will involve you. You are guaranteed to feel better at the conclusion of any scenario knowing that at least you made your opinion known.

The same concept applies to you and the precedence you make your dreams, desires, wants, needs, likes and dislikes. It's similar to setting standards for your life, but with a slight difference. When you make yourself your own top priority, you know and believe that your needs are important, you are worthy to receive blessings, and you are deserving of the positive results from opportunities that you have created in your life.

However, you must remember that you place yourself as top priority because only after you care for your own needs, can you successfully care for others in your life. The people who depend on you may include your children, a spouse, or your parents, and others. To operate at optimum levels, your mind, spirit and body must all be at their peak. When you put yourself first, you are concerned with all areas of your life and filling any voids in areas that are lacking.

 Sometimes making yourself top priority may be as simple as receiving a massage, a manicure or taking out a few moments of quiet time for yourself to clear your thoughts and relax your body. Other times it may be as extensive as requesting professional assistance with personal matters, gathering a support team to help you with a dilemma or changing your schedule so as not to stress yourself. Whatever the case may be, realize that making yourself your own top priority does not mean ignoring others or giving yourself unnecessary or undue importance. It simply means making sure that you are in the best possible condition to experience life while striving to reach your peak potential and sharing the empowering benefits with loved ones.

Do Black Women Have an Attitude?

It was not until my teenage years that I realized my mom was not a superhero. When I was a young child, she had the innate ability to change her total persona from an easy going, soft spoken, kind hearted woman to a feisty, quick witted, and sarcastic, pit bull; all within a matter of seconds. With the latter qualities she could handle any situation that confronted her or deal with any person that upset her at that moment.

She would sometimes warn me that she was about to do her quick change, as if I could somehow tip off the person who she was about to 'bestow' her wrath. "Don't let me start actin' a fool up in here" she would tell me. "They don't want to see me actin' like a --." I would quietly and anxiously await the results of an escalated situation, realizing the person on the receiving end had no idea what they had gotten themselves into. To this day, anyone who purposely *or* inadvertently mishandles my mom or her belongings will be a bit more 'enlightened' afterwards. Cashiers- who are reluctant to exchange an item for her, carpenters- that may take too long with renovations on her home, or waitresses and hotel personnel- who confuse orders will all tell you, "Don't mess with that lady right there!"

Friends and family are quick to remind me that I look just like my mom and share her same demeanor. So, it is not much of a leap for me to don the same cape and superhero tendencies when problems present themselves. Sure, I understand the bias in thinking that the attitudes I, perhaps, possess is purely an extension of my temper, which gets shorter as I grow older. Of course, the tow truck driver, my ex, and my nosey neighbor, all had it coming.

Many years ago, while having legitimate debates, disagreements, or whatever you want to call them, with my husband at the time, he would occasionally blurt out, "That's why I can't stand you Black women!" However, he was an extremist. He hated the fact that I read 'Waiting to Exhale,' a book authored by a black woman, about black women. It was a book that contained attitude, and then some. In fact, in one heated quarrel I recall, he very pointedly exclaimed that his *next* relationship would be with a Caucasian woman. I knew we weren't going to last after *that* conversation. Oh, I did mention that he is a black man, didn't I?

In fact, I've heard a few black men state that they do not want to deal with a black woman's 'funky attitude' as a reason why they no longer pursue them for relationships. I'm sure, with that mind-set, Thelma from 'Goodtimes' would definitely give any one of them a run for their money.

Are these particular men not sympathetic in understanding the thoughts and feelings of black women or are they merely tired of the attitude they've received so many years previous from their own mother, sisters, cousins and aunts? Or, interestingly, how *do* they deal with relatives that project such attitude? Do they label them too, invisible, as they have resolved to do as concerns other black females? Maybe they delightfully put up with them, that is, until the family reunion is over.

 I can't help wondering though; do all black women have this attitude? Is this 'attitude' something that is learned or is it a survival mode that we regress to, to deal with life and it's twists and turns? Why does it seem some women cannot 'turn it off'? Are they just angry all the time, or do they genuinely feel threatened? Pose the question, "Do black women have an attitude?" to anyone, and it is sure to spark a lively debate or at the very least, a spicy, opinionated conversation.

Black Woman

Each day I live, I learn who a black woman is
you cannot define her, simply by words

Sight, smell and sound must all be used, to infuse
the depth of her character

I understand who a black woman is by how deeply she loves
She has deferred simple pleasures to become an accommodating
spirit

I appreciate who a black woman is by what she has sacrificed
because she has selflessly considered another

When surrounded by inadequacy, she has proved herself capable.

Historically, the black woman has been tweaking her place in society
for years,

Brazen, as she refused to move her seat.
Quick witted when she cautiously freed slaves,
Outspoken when she spoke the truth,
Nurturing as she nursed her owner's child

The mystery of the black woman is that she is a living, breathing
contradiction,
She is delicate, but her spirit is not easily broken
She is strong willed, yet yielding to love

The gift of the black woman is the ability to carry the world on her
shoulders
while facing her fears

The black woman is everlasting,
The black woman is exacting.

I am proud to be a black woman

As a Woman

Fantastically, I am a woman
Dramatically, I have proven

When my surroundings are in ruin
I have the strength to hold it together

I am the mother who comforts her child
I am the sister who is piercingly blunt
I am the wife who has gained your trust

I am the grandmother who has watched her seeds grow
Into a firmly planted root, a family with extended branches

Stems, and certainly leaves, that appear to have knees
Bended at my side, acknowledging my praise

Because at the end of my days,
I have done all I can,
As a woman

Raecine Tyes

A Taste of My Reality

Savor the flavor; it might not last too long
I've been caught singing that same old song
Just like a Negro spiritual
Was it supposed to inspire me or lift me higher?

I must've missed that part

I entered on the second verse
You keep saying things are going to get better
But it seems like they're steadily getting worse
I know, I know
I'm supposed to keep my head up like Tupac was saying
I've had it bowed for a while now
Because I've been steadily praying

Do you think it will help if I start tithing?

My problems started way back,
Probably when that first cotton seed was sown
I've been placed in a class all of my own
Sometimes I've been called "girl,"
Even though I'm full grown
Don't get me wrong, I have been called a queen
But I'm still trying to find my throne

And what's funny- is, as dark as my skin- is
At times,
At times I've become invisible

You know
One time, I was in line
Things were quite fine
Until the cashier looked right past me
He didn't ask me
What he could help me with

Or sometimes I might be walking,

We're not paying attention because one of us is talking
And I know you bumped into me
But the way you glare, its right through me
And- not surprisingly,
You haven't said a word

Although statistically I'm quite popular
Realistically, you'd think that disease and crime wouldn't occur
Unless it existed with me

Or at least that's what the media would lead you to believe
But I know better

I'm progressively digging myself out from the rut I'm in

I've empowered myself!
I've acquired knowledge.
I'm inspired by my sisters!

I've gone from down on my knees scrubbing floors
To being placed on corporate boards
I was told not to own a book because reading was against the rules
Now I'm the principal at your children's schools
I was the object of your torment, for which there was no cause
Today I prominently write and even enforce laws
I was silenced, ridiculed and made to think I was weak
Now people line up and pay to hear me speak
You thought entertainment was my only claim to fame
Did you fail to notice the three letters at the end of my name?
In the past I've been given, and I've settled, for what was left
But now I take a deep breath, because I'm so blessed!

However, at times I pause
And tears fall
I'm appreciative of the position in which I've been placed
But those same tears are for ancestors gone and the struggle they
faced

I'm not looking for sympathy
Although I do demand your respect

Raecine Tyes

You won't catch me waiting by my mailbox for a two hundred year old check

Everything I do is for my advancement
So all the years my ancestors fought won't be wasted

And please,
Don't say you understand where I'm coming from
Unless my reality you've tasted

Read... It's Good for You!

A fun and popular survey, which was passed around Facebook, asked people to list 25 things about themselves. The purpose was for old friends and new acquaintances alike to learn more about you. One of the first things that came to my mind was that I loved to read motivational and inspirational books. I stated, "I spend a lot of time at any bookstore and I spend even more at the counter." Books are a priceless gift. You can learn, travel, or be entertained, solely by reading. You can get ideas, start a new career, save money, learn a language or merely pass time by reading a book. I don't like to hear people say they hate to read. To me, it's as if they are saying, "I hate to learn, travel, explore, be entertained, experience different cultures, and live!" All those things can be done through books. Read, and then take what you've read to the next level in your own life. Advance your knowledge about any topic, even before you take a class, simply by reading.

I can remember when I was seven months pregnant visiting the Hartford Public Library along with my daughter, who was 3 years old at the time. We both carried as many books as our bags would hold. Step by step, I waddled up and down the large stone staircase of the old building that was under renovation. I remember what I must've looked like, and it wouldn't be a stretch to think I was a new circus act.

We'd regularly check out children's books; always as many as we could possibly carry, as if we'd never have a chance to visit the library again. However, I remember my mother doing the same for me and my brother when we were little. I didn't realize that I was creating a true bookworm of my daughter, who now divulges any book given to her at an amazingly fast pace. I've always tried to instill in my children the importance of gathering their own information, about anything. *Reading gives you the opportunity to be proactive about your education.* You don't have to, and you won't have to accept just anything that another person tells you.

If reading is a chore because it's difficult for you, then practice at a pace that is comfortable for you. Underline or circle words that you don't understand or can't pronounce. Look them up in a dictionary or research them in a thesaurus to find words with similar meaning. Other things you can do are read with another person to make it enjoyable. Start a book club and read with friends who have the same interests. Never underestimate books and the knowledge you can gain from reading them.

Passionately Speaking

 In high school, some of my teachers had to scold me for talking too much. In one class, a teacher literally moved my desk to every possible location around the room where he thought I wouldn't strike up a conversation with an innocent victim. Unfortunately, I didn't discriminate. I'd talk to anyone and everyone about everything. Looking back, I just loved talking, period.

My earliest job through a school work study program was as an interviewer conducting 20 minute telephone surveys with executives about digital phone systems. My supervisor charted progress on a white board that displayed each person's daily and weekly stats. I exceeded, surpassing employees that had been on the job for years; That is, until I had to get a handful of wisdom teeth surgically removed. Needless to say, my numbers went down the drain after that. I also surpassed fellow seasoned co-workers as a car salesperson, selling a record number of *very* high mileage vehicles that had to be secured with 20% cash down payment. I'm not too proud about that gig. Every sales job I undertook was a breeze, probably because I had the 'gift of gab'.

 My point is that communication was an unrealized passion of mine early in life. I always hear, "If you love what you do in life, the money will come." Yeah, well the money came, and it went right passed me. I didn't have the smarts to consider a long term career in communication. Hence, the dead end jobs. If the teacher that moved me around the room would have made a list of careers in communication, then assigned an oral report to me on the topic, I would have loved that!

Recognize what your passions and talents are, then focus attention on them while adding emotion and positive energy. By doing this you will easily create infinite opportunities for yourself. Sustain excitement in your life by incorporating your passions into everything you do. If your passion is something that involves skill, get educated so that you can be the best at whatever you love doing anyway.

Got Stress?

Imagine the following stressful scenarios; a grandparent dies, you and your children survive a bad wreck that totals your new car, you move from a townhome into a house, you end a 3 year long relationship; you are the money broker for an 8 figure deal. Now, consider that each one of these takes place on the same weekend. Well, that's exactly what happened to me. I dealt with each circumstance as best as I knew how, practically and systematically. However the way my body handled it was totally different. After about two weeks, I started to notice my heart racing at short intervals. Attributing it to caffeine I perhaps had earlier in the day, I didn't pay it much attention.

However, when my racing heart turned more into a pounding in my chest, I knew something was definitely wrong. I'd do everything to try and calm myself, including long hot showers, sipping herbal tea or relaxing by laying still. When I was well rested and my symptoms persisted without the presence of any stimulants, I went the emergency room. As the triage nurse took my vitals, she began to ask me "Have you had anything with caffeine, any stimulants, any drugs of *any* kind?" My answer to each was, "No, no, no ma'am!" I knew there was a problem when she hollered out to the other nurse, "We're going to need a full package on this one!" What I later found out, after they quickly admitted me is that my heart rate reached 140….while I was sitting completely still!

During that hospital stay, I had so many wires hooked up to me that my own children were frightened. After completing numerous stress tests, ekgs, and a cat scan, I was told that there was nothing wrong with me. I was however, given a prescription for an anti acid, to reduce the acid in my stomach, no doubt the result of stress. That untimely visit to the hospital was enough to scare me straight. From that point on, I paid attention to every signal my body gave me. From slight tension in my shoulders to a mild headache or just a general feeling of uneasiness; I was aware of it all and quickly made myself relax at the first sign of discomfort.

Even though I dealt with my stress factors in a pragmatic way, I realized that I had to take it one step further and focus on solutions rather than dwelling on the problems I encountered. Also, exercise became a vital part of my weekly routine rather than a passive option. Healthier, lighter meals which included a large portion of vegetables made me feel more energetic and alive.

It's a scary feeling to feel your heart pounding as if you've just been in a triathlon and in actuality you haven't lifted a finger. To avoid coming anywhere close to that happening again, I drastically changed my lifestyle for the better. I now experience a more peaceful existence, understanding that every problem, scenario or circumstance, whether good or bad will be taken care of in due time. I focus on the positive in any situation to prevent my mind from spiraling into a sea of negativity in which worst case scenarios are highlighted. Simple exercises performed when the onset of tension emerged, helped tremendously. Of course, if you have an extraordinary amount of stress that you can't deal with on your own, it's best to visit your doctor. Otherwise, a few basic tips that I've mentioned can hopefully help to manage it before it even gets that far.

Keep Proving Me Wrong

I am, because of you
I have endured, because of your love

When I had nowhere to turn
You provided for me

When I didn't know where to go
You guided me

What I thought was tragedy
You said was my lesson.
Indeed, a now realized blessing

Powerfully, you uplifted me
Wisdom, your gift to me

I thought I was weak
You proved me wrong

So with all my strength
I praise you
I beg you

Keep loving me
Keep guiding me
Keep blessing me

Keep proving me wrong.

Homeless

Homelessness can be an overnight thing or a gradual one; for me, it was a little of both. Trusting in a man and a relationship that he and I both assumed was going to end in marriage, I moved myself and my two children to Maryland. Only six hours south of Connecticut, the move wasn't too bad, but it was still a big adjustment. While he stayed in a cramped one room condo with his family, my children and I were fortunate to room with a middle aged, single mother in a 4 bedroom home a few miles away. After all, we both decided this would be a temporary situation until we saved money, got married and found a home of our own.

 I paid significantly reduced rent for occasionally babysitting two children who lived in my home. In addition, I worked a full time job as a retail store manager. With my beau supporting me, things were a breeze. That is, until my landlord/roommate decided a few months later that she was moving to Baltimore, which was about 30 minutes north of where we were now located. She asked if I would consider moving with them. After all, she was used to having a live in sitter and probably grew accustomed to me cooking all the time, which I loved to do. I politely told her I'd think about it, but the more I did I knew it wasn't going to happen. *"Baltimore?!* I'm not going to no *Baltimore!"* I must have repeated that to everyone I spoke to in the next few days. Ultimately I scrambled around to find another 'perfect living situation' which did not exist.

After two failed roommate attempts in less than two months, my quest for the perfect 'roomie' ended with me calling the police. He was the most unlikely predator, a much older man that allowed us to rent a part of his home. However, his intentions on what type of roommate he wanted soon became brutally apparent. When he realized he was alone in his fantasies; unbeknown to me, he literally packed up every last one of our belongings. He piled everything we had into a minivan he owned and basically told us to go fetch them.

My relationship, which went sour weeks earlier, for its own set of heartbreaking reasons, was then reignited out of necessity. Of course, he was happier than a kid in a candy store, because now I needed his help. I eventually moved in with him; in an apartment he recently obtained. Though in the interim, I spent my last paycheck staying in hotels and desperately searched for a place to live. I did all I could to find somewhere, but my meager salary and the high cost of living in that area was a bad combination. He was my last resort, and moving back to Connecticut, burdening my family, was not an option for me.

At that time, I was a student at University of Phoenix in Maryland and I concurrently attended a technical computer class. One of my classmates was generous enough to let us stay in her home for a few days, but she too had a full plate that I refused to add to. Fortunately, her husband worked for a high quality hotel chain, so we were able to stay quite comfortably, at some of the nicest spots in Maryland, D.C. and Virginia paying less than a third of what a room regularly cost. My children and I spent about two weeks hopping from hotel to hotel. We didn't forgo the one or two nights in the car though, distressing as it was. Because of one catalyst, I lost a roommate, my job and regretfully returned to a bad relationship, which eventually got worse.

Knowing that I could no longer subject myself or my kids to the relationship, I prepped them for weeks, helping them to understand what was going on. I decided we were going to move. I saved money and planned exactly how and what we were going to do. I don't like drama, so we would move the moment he left for work, at 4 a.m. on a weekday morning. With the exception of his items, the kids and I cleared out everything we owned, within minutes! That afternoon, I desperately wanted to know his reaction to what I had done, mainly to validate that our relationship was over beyond any doubt. I remember talking with him on the phone and after he sobbingly said he wished he could've said goodbye face to face, he added, "Raecine, you even took the shower curtain?" in the most pitiful voice he could muster.

During those two years in Maryland, it seemed as if time was moving backwards for me. My experience was like a twilight zone. I permitted my circumstances to push me around, and it happened at an *extremely* rapid pace. I now knew just how the little silver ball in a pinball game felt, jolted every which way, without any advance warning. I was worth more than what I was allowing in my life, and more importantly my children deserved much better.

If you wake up one day and you recognize you are in a situation that is physically, mentally, or spiritually unhealthy; do whatever you must to get out and away from that person! Whether it is a person you are in a relationship with, an associate or a friend. Of course, there will be strong feelings involved, you may even feel like life won't be the same without that person; well, fortunately it *won't* be the same. Yes, you may love them, but it may be best if you love them from a distance. Things will most likely get better. I learned the hard way.

From personal experience I learned that negative people are like parasites that need to feed on another person, a host, for survival. Negative energy from other people will drain you, weaken you, and depress you. It can also make you physically tired. If children are involved, they will absorb some of the effects, although you may not see it immediately. I can only pray that my children weren't affected by what I'd put them through.

Bills

Can you sympathize?
Do you see the pain in my eyes?
It's no surprise,
That most of my stressin'
I'm finally confessin'
is because of bills

Lack of money
or shall I say funds?
Well it doesn't matter because either one
means I don't have any money in the bank
And that's not fun
I won't say I'm broke, because I do have a job
but it doesn't work
So, maybe my job is broke

Do you have any suggestions?
A quick fix maybe
I've heard lately
that I'm not the only one in this situation
Perhaps a simple negotiation
with the collector on the phone
Do you think he can tell if I'm home?

Because if I see his number I won't answer

Speaking of answer, I been praying about this
and I haven't gotten any response yet
But I'm not going to fret,
I'm not going to let these bills get me all upset

'Cause in time, it's all going to be handled
before my furniture gets dismantled,

and… has to go
Or my car gets repoed…
Or …the lights go out

And I'm not talking about Teddy
oh no, now my hands are getting sweaty

But I'm not going to worry
It's not like I'm facing a jury
That's not until next week
For all that stuff the medical did to my credit
I mine as well hang it up and forget it

They already took my tax return
All that hard money I earned
What a lesson I've learned

I need some kind of financial rehab
A makeover for my wallet
this financial mess is affecting my closet
You won't find anything new in there
Not even new shoes
I been hittin' the Goodwill,
All my stuff is used

But I'm going to make it through this though

I'm going to cut down on some expenses
Stop buying things that are senseless
and be relentless, about where my money goes
Before I'm rent less

I'm going to work a few extra hours
and maybe take a class
because my money's moving slow
but these bills are moving fast

When all is said and done
It's all in what God wills
Cause lord knows, I'm tired of asking my momma
to help me pay my bills

Raecine Tyes

Cinnamon Rain

I categorically denied that all the negativity was real
thinking that if I numbed my emotions, I wouldn't be able to feel

Every time you said you were sorry, I gave you a second chance
thinking it would enhance, our bond, which was weakening

I tried to make us stronger,
stretch what we had out a little longer

Ignoring the facts, in fact
the more I prolonged it

the more love left
and what was left
was an emptiness

that was there all along

I'm still trying to understand what happened to us
Was it a matter of trust?

I thought I gained that, so that's not to blame
what's a shame, is for the sake of your name

you insanely and profanely defamed me
in front of your family

That's something I didn't deserve

That was unexpected
You treated me like a suspect
whatever was wrong could've been corrected
it's just that

right now I'm hurting and I don't think you care
remember the time I cared for you, when no one else was there?

It's only been a few months, we were supposed to last forever
So maybe we shouldn't have been together, Never!
You were always saying, "Whatever"

Evidence of no empathy, for the relationship that we had,
Had we stayed together,

Things would have deteriorated,
badly

I was madly

In love with you
don't you remember?

How we used to sit outside till morning, until the dew came?
The air, it smelled so sweet
We called it cinnamon rain

My Kids

I'm about to go crazy
And I don't think I'm lazy

But am I supposed to jump every time my kids say "ma"
And are my kids the only ones that when I call them, they answer
"hah?"

And maybe my volume is down low, because I been repeating my
self a lot
I said I been repeating myself a lot.
Did you hear what I said?!
I've been repeating myself… let me stop

And yes, I did name them, with all the joy in the world,
but sometimes I happen to call them "little boy" and "little girl"

From the way my family acts, you'd think they were royalty
Well that royal heritage must have skipped right passed me

I will say, both of mine, seem to like every vegetable
But their choice is clothing now, that is definitely questionable

And if you have at least two, it's always the other who started the
bickering
And when you're disciplining one, the other one is always
snickering

And can yours remember the date, day and time you're supposed to
take them to Chuckee Cheese?
Please.

But when it comes to something you said
maybe like, why didn't you make your bed?
Then their memory goes dead?

I'm convinced my kids will be great journalists, attorneys or private
eye,

because when I answer any question with " no"
they determinedly ask why

And my daughter, she's at the age, she doesn't want me to give her
my hair dos
Even though as a cosmetologist, I've gotten rave reviews
She always wants something new
And have you seen the cost of children's clothes and shoes?

You would think it's cheaper because they're smaller?
By no means am I a baller

I'm just a single mother trying to make my ends meet at the end of
the week
Put clothes on their back, and give them something to eat
And my kids *always* want something sweet

You know I used to give them each 50 cents to massage my neck
and rub my feet
But at some point they learned the value of a dollar

So now they won't bother
for less than 5 or 6
Yeah, my kids got tricks
They think they slick

But I can't ask for much more
I have two lovely kids that I adore

One son, one daughter, they're really no bother
But it figures, they each, look just like their father

The Blessing of Children

Recently, while talking to one of my friends on the telephone, I overheard her calling out to her one year old son. In an attempt to fend him out of trouble, she cried, "Get over here little boy!" I chuckled. "So, you're calling him little boy now?" I asked. "Oh yes," she replied, "He's been 'little boy' for about two months now." We both laughed. As a mother of two school age children, I realized that she was about to experience the joys of toddler hood and the mischievousness that accompanies it.

As a child, I remember my mother calling my brother 'little boy' and I often times find myself referring to my own children as 'little boy' and 'little girl' when they seem to purposely frustrate me with inappropriate actions. The attractive and thoughtful names I picked for them when they were babies, somehow are inadequate and just don't seem to fit the occasion when I'm disciplining them.

Raising children is a blessing, learning experience and challenge all in one. Children can bring out multiple dimensions in your personality that you never knew existed. I consider myself to be very easy going and laid back; but at times I have a feeling that my children are *deliberately* trying to drive me crazy! They appear to be determined to complete a mission that isn't covert by any means. For example, in the process of writing this book, their most rambunctious behavior emerged whenever I was working quietly. I'm conscious that their antics are most likely due to them vying for my attention, which I probably over indulge them with in the first place. They usually bombard me with loud, thoughtless chatter, a barrage of meaningless questions or obnoxious physical movement involving anything from dance without any apparent music to bickering between them that eventually leads to fighting.

In contrast, each and every school year; they both achieve honor roll status, best behaved in class and student of the month and student of the year for their respective grade levels, so I know that *it is* possible for them to act like they have some sense. And for their accomplishments I am an extremely proud parent. I make this well known by thoroughly embarrassing my children with hoots and howls, whistling and shouts of my adoration of them at ribbon and certificate ceremonies, graduations, school assemblies, or whenever and wherever I get the chance to do so.

As a single parent, raising children can sometimes feel overwhelming when confronted with financial or emotional issues that affect the family. In fact, I'm sure that two parent households are equally faced with concerns that are trying as well. However, consistent prayer with my children and constant communication between us has been our stronghold. The combination of the two is vital in reiterating my message to my son and daughter that as a family, we are a team strengthened by a spiritual bond. By openly discussing issues they may come across at school, with peers, and matters that may be weighing on their mind, I hope to stave off problems in their teen years and beyond. I've kept my children empowered by reminding them that they are capable to be successful at whatever they choose to do and that they are only limited by their own belief system. I've made reading an integral part of their life so that they have the ability to acquire knowledge for themselves, rather than waiting on another person for answers.

My son and daughter, although only 12 and 9 years of age, at the time of this printing, can each prepare and cook a full meal, wash and fold clothes, and clean our home to my specifications. I don't believe in babying a child so that they are unprepared and helpless in a world ready to catch them off guard to their detriment. At the opposite end of the spectrum, we spend enjoyable recreational time together such as riding go carts, swimming, riding bikes, movies and family fun time.

As an adult, I now appreciate the relentless training on the part of my parents for my spiritual and physical benefit. I am grateful for the endless hours of hard work they put in to present me and my siblings with sufficient clothing and an abundance of food in a clean, warm home. Also, I can especially relate to and understand what I considered to be nagging by my parents at that time, and why not? Now, I sound just like them.

I Aspire

Time wasted, money down the drain
Its insane, how laziness in my brain,
causes a simple refrain
from action

Procrastination
A dirty word that halts progress
and stalls success,
It stops me from being my best
Unable to move on to what's next
I become perplexed

Without letting it fully arrest me
I began to create my own destiny
My family and friends invest in me
By pledging their support

I aspire

And furthermore I've become a source of
inspiration
A reason for exhalation
Because I've accomplished
what my mind said couldn't be done
It was a case of mind over matter
And in this case, my spirit won

I am joyful

I'm rejoicing in the face of my obstacles
Because I've placed them behind me
With only remnants of my past to remind me
And I've now become unstoppable

Hopeless

Sometimes I feel hopeless
Yet I, hold my head up
hoping no one will notice

Refraining from conversation
so I won't have to force a smile
I'd rather walk a mile

than to deal with the pain it causes me
Negative energy is calling me

But I don't answer

I choose to stay focused
and strengthen my abilities
Rather than fall back on bad tendencies

I procrastinate

I'm my own worst enemy
I desire a new beginning
but it's going to be the end of me

So, all the strength within my soul I muster
Because I must
leave a legacy
There's no leaving to chance, my destiny

My future has already begun
I aspire
and build
on the web of goals I've spun

Raecine Tyes

Procrastination is a Dirty Word

I've paid out hundreds of dollars in car maintenance and overdue fees; I've missed important events, appointments, experienced an armful of regrets and even carried around a few extra pounds, all thanks to my ability to procrastinate. I could've ended bad relationships much quicker, been further along in my career and made substantially more money, if only I hadn't befriended procrastination. When speaking about procrastination, I feel I should be giving some type of eye opening statistic on how harmful it is, as if it were some type of dirty crime reported on the nightly news.

Experts say that procrastination is due to feeling as if doing the actual deed of whatever it is you need to accomplish will cause you mental anguish or pain. Well, taking action and succeeding with everything on life's to do list *has* to be a lot less painful than what I've endured in the past, *due to* me procrastinating. This is especially true when it comes to kicking out money that you really don't have to spend or realizing that you've wasted valuable time.

An embarrassing but true example of how this works is the day I was pulled over on my way to work. Usually this would not be a big deal, however, when past traffic violations are forgotten and unpaid, it makes matters worse. This particular day, my procrastination slapped me in the face. I wasn't aware that because of my slow execution, or just plain non action to pay a previous ticket, driver services suspended my license and revoked my car registration. So instead of just one lousy unpaid ticket, I was faced with a ticket three times as much as the original, reinstatement fees for my license and registration, towing fees, and not to mention I was docked for being late to work that day.

The only good thing about procrastination is that you have the power to stop it at anytime; it takes willpower though. Procrastination is destructive because it allows you to accept excuses for yourself and renders you unproductive. By procrastinating, you are consenting to sub standards for your life, never reaching your full potential because in that state of mind action is deemed optional, not essential. Anyone confronting procrastination has to deal with it head on, almost like an attendee at an AA meeting, using steps, whatever they may be, to combat it. I do know that first and foremost, you must realize that you have a problem with procrastination. Abandon all thoughts of thinking whatever it may be that needs doing can be put off until a later date. Do it now!

If it helps, make a list of important steps, or chores that have to be completed, whether they are daily or weekly. Carry the list with you everywhere you go and highlight priority items. Do not check off any item until it is actually completed. Remind yourself that you will be a much better person after you have accomplished the task and even get support from a family member or friend if necessary. The embarrassment of not completing an action should help get you into gear and put your mind on autopilot to finish subsequent lists with ease. Also, remember to reward yourself for every improvement you make in battling procrastination. You can do it!

Choose Your Words Wisely

My brother and I were talking the other day about a mutual friend who senselessly repeated harsh obscenities to a female coworker, which another *male* coworker spoke just moments earlier. Needless to say, our friend was fired almost immediately while his buddy went unscathed. My brother and I couldn't help but shake our heads in disbelief. The words that he repeated were so horrible, that common sense alone should have told him to 'leave it alone.' Our friend obviously didn't learn the lesson that we did in our childhood.

"Just keep your mouth shut. Your mouth is what gets you in trouble." I can still hear my father saying those exact words now; they were the result of me or one of my siblings talking out of term, perhaps in a disrespectful manner. Those two sentences however, were my father's either warning or final say, depending on if he'd already popped us on our mouth or not. After which, we'd begrudgingly wipe our mouths off as if we could magically wipe away where he'd hit us. Then we'd mumble, almost silently, under our breaths, of our disgust for the discipline we'd just received. It was a lesson that stuck with us until today though, because my brother and I simultaneously agreed that our friend just didn't know how to keep his mouth shut.

How many times have politicians, teachers, entertainers, employers, coworkers, professional athletes, friends, husbands, wives or children all gotten themselves into trouble for not being able to control their speech? All you have to do is turn on your local news to hear examples of how someone's words, racist remarks, sexist language, senseless comments, or biased opinions got them into trouble. And with the technology of personal recorders, video devices and telephones that capture all forms of media, it's easier than ever to catch candid moments from friends or foes.

I definitely understand that freedom of speech has paved a better life for people; however, I'm referring to speech whose only intention is to belittle, harm or damage. Speaking without thinking has gotten many people reprimanded, fired, sued, divorced, in fights or even killed. If everyone would just take a few seconds to think about the impact of what they are about to say before it actually flows out of their mouths, there'd surely be a lot fewer heartache and embarrassment. I have advice for those people who just don't know that sometimes you can think it, but you just can't say it. It is actually the same advice my father gave me, "Just keep your mouth shut!"

My Apologies

You live once, you die once...so,

forgive me
if I don't feed into your negativity.
Although it may be subtle and its real intentions hide
under the guise
of love.

Excuse me
for not restricting myself
to the self limiting standards you'd like to impose on me
I'm striving to reach my full potential and I will do this
regardless
of what you think I am
or am not capable of

I'm sorry
if I don't feed into your "bushwick"
in the past you've said it so quick
that I didnt have a chance to escape it
I'd sit there quietly and humbly listen to every word you'd say
But with my new gained confidence I've realized that within each
day
there is a new way
to express my individuality
so like a stiff drink, take a slow sip of my personality

Don't take it personal
if I don't conform to your clouded perception of me
I know myself better than anyone
So don't feel bad
if I don't take your suggestions
on how I can better be me

I cannot be who you think I am
I have grown into a much wiser person than you remember

Success Looks Good on Me

I cannot be who you want me to be
I refuse to let you stifle the person I truly am
so that you can feel more comfortable in your own skin

If you really care for me, be down with me,
rather than put me down

If you truly love me
support me, encourage me, empower me, inspire me!

Each step I take is intentional
So why do you question my actions?
Whether you understand my vision or not, trust in me
Be there for me

And don't feel bad that, right now
at this moment
I am unapologetically, decidedly and unregretful-ly
doing me!

Haters Aren't Your Motivators

Every time I hear the phrase "Let your haters be your motivators," I want to scream! To me, that is a backward way of thinking. I understand the concept behind the phrase, but it still doesn't make sense to me. Haters, people who secretly crave your downfall, are a source of negative energy and shouldn't even be given a space in your mind, let alone a basis of your inspiration. How can something bad, which exudes negative energy toward you, propel you into positive situations or opportunities? It can't.

I've known of people who laughed at me and my ideas or projects that I've undertaken, including this book. I was furious to think that one particular person had such awful and downright mean things to say about my efforts. My first instinct was to try to place my foot in locations his body could not possibly support. After the initial shock, I had a feeling of wanting to complete my project for the sole purpose of rubbing it in his face and making him feel stupid. When I finally came to my senses, I realized that if I were to write with thoughts of him on my brain, my intentions of inspiring someone would be clouded with negativity. This is not the type of motivation that I needed or wanted to project. It's also much easier to conjure up good outcomes for yourself when you have good intentions.

Similarly, anything done with a negative motivator is not going to have the same results as a project done with love. Just as you can feel tension when walking into a room of angry people, the same is true if you use haters as a source of inspiration for any project. Even though it may sound corny, it's true.

Have you ever reluctantly done something or gone somewhere, during which you had an unforeseen encounter with a friend or associate who surprisingly lifted your spirits and inspired you for whatever reason? That positive, chance meeting may have been so moving to you that you thanked that person and let them know what a positive impact they had on your day. Now, think of the same situation but switch the positive associate with a person who despises you and preys on your downfall. Do you think you'd walk away with the same glowing feeling as the first encounter?

My advice is to avoid haters at all costs. Realize that nothing they have to say is going to benefit or motivate you. Their negative energy will only drain you and make you feel worse than when you began. If your haters happen to be a close friend or relative, avoid disclosing your visions or goals with them. Try to recognize why it is that they have such harsh feelings toward your success and if it can't be resolved, have as little interaction with such people. Our days are filled with enough tension and stress than to have one more negative factor to weigh us down. You will feel much better when your haters are not in your line of sight which hinders you from focusing on your vision, whether it is your relationship with god, your goals or a successful family life.

Me

People love what I write and they don't even like poetry
And just like Floetry
If you say *Yes* that's cool,
because a Maybe is a *No* to me
I invite all spoken word artists, poets and rappers to take a go at me
They never knew me before
but now they know of me

My facebook friends keep on poking me
Haters constantly provoking me
Brown nosers grab a hold of my ego,
they keep on stroking me
I don't take things too serious;
it must be the joke in me

My entrepreneurial spirit powers the go in me
My shameless promotion, that's just the show in me
I write what I live which provides the flow in me
I try my best to inspire, even if unknowingly

Now you're checking the heat, Cause I'm making it hotter
So negative people won't even bother

I'm a beast and I'm about to unleash
All the talent I've hidden for years
Now when I express myself tears of joy
Fall, as leaves do, in the Fall

The wisdom I've gained
It's almost frightening
How inspiration hits me like a flash of lightning

I'm flirting with success, but I'm ready to tango
I'm so, so, so....into this totally, been spittin' this poetry
Like it's the last thing on earth,
It's my time to shine
I'm going for what it's worth

Success Looks Good on Me

Hungry

You ain't hungry like I am
I'm dieing to prove myself and show off my abilities
its killing me, how willy- nillingly
others claim to be

ain't nothing left but fame for me
this ain't no game to me
I got two kids to feed
by *any* means (thanks Malcolm)

Hungry

If you want to make it in life, you've got to stay hungry! Hungry for whatever it is you are aspiring to accomplish. Whether you want to have a successful business, exciting career, top grades in school or a beautiful family, it all takes work. You can't sit around and wait for someone to hand you anything, especially not your own dreams. It'll never happen! Have you ever seen any student land a sports scholarship merely because he daydreams of becoming a star player one day? Do you know of any surgeons who are top in their field without going to medical school? Perhaps you know of a successful attorney that never once studied law? I doubt he'd receive any phone calls from potential clients. It would be ridiculous to think that a person would take any one of these people serious.

It never ceases to amaze me how easily people give up on goals because of minor setbacks or temporary distractions. Too many times people allow unfavorable situations to hinder them from becoming or doing what they set out to accomplish. And even more often than that, low self confidence usually squashes a good idea or aspiration before it even goes into the planning stages. I've experienced this personally even up to the point of completing this book. Every type of distraction possible presented itself, but it was up to me to categorize each with its own level of importance, and from that point I had to either deal with the situation or ignore it.

Distractions can come in all shapes, sizes and forms. They can also appear as acquaintances, friends or family members. Sometimes it's simply a person or a situation that promises loads but fails to deliver. Although at the time it may seem like a stepping stone to your success, ultimately it's just a bridge to nowhere. How do I know? Throughout the years I've allowed financial difficulties, relationships and circumstances to stand in the way of me obtaining success on a large scale. I am however a firm believer that everything under the sun has a reason for happening and occurring in our life. Therefore, even if you didn't receive instant gratification from a particular relationship, opportunity or experience, use it to your advantage as a learning lesson. Take the positive from each situation or person you encounter in life.

Sometimes the realization of the lesson may take months or years to present itself. Be ready and accept the lesson when it does appear. In the meantime, if you do find yourself in a situation which is counterproductive or distracting and doesn't align itself with the vision you have for yourself, distance yourself from it!

Don't let any obstacles dampen your desire to reach your goals. Continuously and consistently strive to reach your full potential. If you have reached a level of success, never be content or settled. Stay hungry to always be your best!

Go For It!

In order to be successful, you will have to be flexible to new ideas and open to new experiences. Saying no before you know the benefit of any scenario or because you don't want to move from out of your comfort zone will greatly decrease the amount of good opportunities you encounter in your life. If you have the opportunity to travel, take it! If you are able to educate yourself with classes, do it! If someone invites you to learn a new activity, learn it! Life can be unpredictable, so if you are ever afforded the opportunity to experience positive, new things, go for it!

Have you ever watched a sporting event on your television, one which had you jumping out of your seat because of the excitement it brought forth within you? Imagine being a attendee at that same game, it would no doubt be an awesome feeling ten times beyond just watching it on a two dimensional television screen. Instead of adjusting the volume on your set and perhaps playing with the color hues, you'd actually be there to feel, smell and breathe everything happening within that moment. If you wanted to, you'd actually be able to take note of the expression on each and every individual's face in the stadium, or perhaps walk up to them! Furthermore, instead of just looking at a bird's eye view of the players from a camera man's angle, imagine being on the playing field with them, bumping into them as they run frantically to make a goal. Finally, take a deep breath and smell all the different smells, whether good or bad, radiating in the air. All of these different sensory stimuli can't be duplicated by sitting on your butt at home.

Just like everyday life, the only way to truly enjoy it and all the different aspects there are to it, you must be willing to take chances, be flexible and open to what it offers. Think back to a time when you may have had an opportunity to try something or go somewhere, but because you may have been a bit fearful, shy or reluctant you didn't accept the offer. Would you do it again if you had the chance? Instead of saying, "If only I had of..." you would've at least known the outcome of the experience and now been able to share with others what you experienced. Take a chance, go for it!

Step Up Your Game

If you've been working towards a goal and it appears as if you aren't making progress, or results just aren't coming fast enough, then maybe its time for you to step up your game. Stepping up your game requires you to do even more than what you are currently doing. Assess your situation then figure a way to double up on your efforts. This may require you to make twice as many phone calls to make that sale, increase the amount of money you're saving for that purchase, or put more time into a stagnant project. Whatever your situation, don't give up because the momentum has slowed. On the contrary, pick up the pace and see advancements faster by stepping up your game.

 I wanted to lose a few extra pounds this year so I started an exercise regimen and ate lighter meals. I even had the assistance of a personal trainer. For weeks I put forth what I thought was sufficient effort to lose weight. Eventually, I ended up trying to convince myself that my scale was broken. It hardly moved and when it did, it moved in the wrong direction! I was actually gaining more weight.

After fooling myself, and unsuccessfully trying to fool my family with all the diet talk and exercise paraphernalia, I decided it was time to step up my game. Instead of the occasional walk around the neighborhood once or twice a week, I decided I would walk, not only every day, but twice daily. Rather than doing crunches and working on my abs whenever I got a notion to do them, I put myself on a daily routine and did four times as many than my trainer required. I doubled my workouts and pushed myself to do more than I previously did. The results were almost immediate! I finally started to see real weight loss.

Regardless of the level of success you've achieved in life, I'm challenging you to step up your game. Do or become more! Don't be satisfied with the aspirations you've already realized. There is always room for improvement. Have you completed a project or reached a certain status quo and you are content with what you've acquired? Well, guess what? The world is in a constant state of change. If you have your feet up, admiring an award you received ten years ago, while rambling about the "good old days"- you'd better wake up! If you're *sitting back*, instead of *stepping up*, you might just get *left out*.

Opposition

True story...

The other day I met with Opposition
And I explained my position
on how I would've been better off without him

I made it clear that I had no time to waste
Because you see, Opposition likes to slower my pace
He loves to get all up in my face

But this time I took note on his tactics
He got tricks like gymnastics
and when I'm feeling fantastic
that's when he hits me

And his relevancy on any matter at hand doesn't matter
Because he doesn't care and he wants to share
those exact same sentiments of apathy
Especially, when he sees me making advances

He sees I took, and didn't wait for chances
He sees me inspiring, rather than aspiring all by myself
He sees me letting go of the weak mind of poverty
and putting a claim on the mind of wealth
He sees me striving to reach my full potential at all means
He sees me creating a vision for my life
rather than just dreaming dreams

So I asked him, "Opposition... what more do you want from me??!
Because you're clearly not welcome in my life!! You come
unannounced,
unwelcomed, unwarranted, And that just ain't right!"
His answers were weak, silly at best
But he refuses to rest

He continues to bother me and lingers in the past
with an exclamation point on everything he does

Raecine Tyes

But I learned a long time ago to let go of... 'What was'

I plan for the future and stay flexible, with all my goals in sight
Because with Opposition
it's always a never ending fight!

Plan B

If something doesn't go as you hoped for, don't panic, don't worry yourself over it, and whatever you do, don't give up! Just go to Plan B. Do you know how many times I've had projects, jobs, or relationships that went hay wire? I don't have enough fingers, toes or teeth, for that matter, to count every scenario in my life that didn't go as I planned. If I let all the failures in my life stop me in my tracks, that's right where I'd be...standing in my own tracks, alone, stagnant, not making any progress at all. I've heard many times that you must experience failures to reach success, which I believe is partially true. You may fail, however, you only fail if you stop trying or if you don't have a Plan A, B, C, D or E! As long as you are willing to be persistent, determined and become unstoppable, then you will always know that such failures are temporary.

Having a Plan B is more than just being flexible. Someone who is flexible has the ability to move and go with the flow when something abrupt happens to halt their progress. In comparison, having a Plan B makes allowances for those instances even *before* they happen. With Plan B you are prepared in advance and you don't have to make decisions while still trying to deal with the drama of whatever it is that put your original plan out of commission. Of course you may not be prepared to deal with every little thing that pops up, but if you've been working on a project that you've poured considerable time, money or energy into, you want to make sure that you see a fruitful end to all of your efforts.

Testimony to my words can be traced back only a few years earlier to an event that was to be my first huge production. I was excited and motivated about an expo I'd been planning and promoting for about a year. I was fortunate to locate a sponsor that was just as eager as me to promote the event I designed. My sponsor, an independent record label located in New York, poured a considerable amount of money into my ideas to piggyback what I had begun. They immediately ran radio and TV spots which combined, easily reached $12,000. The entertainment which they selected and paid for totaled over $25,000. The venue, which had to be secured in advance, was $10,000 alone. In addition, there were

Raecine Tyes

numerous miscellaneous items. These items had to be purchased weeks before the expo was to take place, such as new posters, flyers and artwork that reflected their company logo. They also paid all the individuals who helped me promote the event and even covered all of my personal expenses which included my rent and car repairs!

Weeks before the event, things were going as planned. Ads promoting my expo could be seen and heard on radio and TV, each hour just like clockwork. Everything was in place and set to go, or so it seemed. The day before my event was to take place, a power outage, of all things, struck many states on the eastern coast of the United States and Canada! Thousands of people could be seen on the news as they abandoned their vehicles on bridges in New York City; for fear that this outage was a repeat of September 11th. And, it just so happened that most of my vendors were traveling from New York, but because the outage lasted for a couple days, they revoked their involvement in my expo. Although this was a major blow to my event, we continued as usual, keeping all plans in place.

The day of the event came; radio personalities were set and ready to broadcast live. Other personalities, vendors and attendees were there as well. People had traveled from New York and some were still en route. However, the *final* straw was that the sound system, a major component for the event to kick off successfully, had not yet arrived, from New York. Hours went by and still the arrival of the equipment that would make everything possible had not appeared. Because it was such a huge event at a moment's notice, securing and transporting another sound system was not an option. I relied on my sponsors to care for everything, thus I failed to draw up a Plan B if anything of that magnitude was to occur.

In the end, it was up to them to make the decision to post pone the event and forfeit all of the financial obligations they invested. Even though it wasn't a financial blow to my wallet personally, I was devastated! I didn't prepare as well as I thought I had. I didn't consider that after spending thousands of dollars to secure an event to go smoothly, something abrupt like the scenario we faced would wipe out all the time, energy and hard work we all invested.

I'm confident in saying that, that was one of the most expensive and painful learning lessons each of us ever endured. However, that failed attempt was definitely not my last attempt to produce an event of that proportion. Next time I will definitely have a Plan A, B, C, D, E and more if necessary, for what will most likely be an even more spectacular expo than that one I envisioned years ago!

Remember, *whatever visions or goals you have for yourself, don't give up on them because you come across hard times!* When you are creating your vision, write down your Plan B, and be ready when obstacles reveal themselves. Don't wallow in pity over the reasons your initial plan didn't work and do not let other people reason that you should stop your venture because of your temporary setback. *Just keep it movin'!* Quickly change to your next plan of action and keep a positive mind about the results you expect to materialize.

Unstoppable

I've become unstoppable, and my confidence has grown
I'm seeing fruitage from the seeds I've sown
I've taken steps to correct some of the steps I've taken
Lessons from my past influence my decision making

I'm expanding now, exceeding all boundaries
It's imperative that positive people surround me

I've taken notes on my road to success
"Never settle for less, control all stress"
And now I'm feeling the effects of being blessed

I consider the source of advice given to me
So that not only will I be inspired
But you can also get inspiration through me

I'm a new me!

Unstoppable- that's my new title
I'm always active and never sitting idle

I'm glowing, I know, people have told me
Afraid to shine? That was the old me

There are no bounds on what I can do
And no limits to what I can acquire
Because if I didn't have the ability
I certainly wouldn't have the desire

I'm willing to share with anyone
All the knowledge that I've learned
Every talent is a gift from God
That can never be earned

Verbally I express my gratitude
Motivating as many possible
If I can do it, you can too

Success Looks Good on Me

I've overcome all obstacles

Now I've risen higher
To heights I've never seen
I've accomplished goals toward my vision,
A vision, which originally was just a dream

Raecine Tyes

Don't Let the 'Experts' Fool You

Experts; it's a safe bet to assume that you've experienced them at one point or time in your life. I've given the term 'Experts' to the people who don't have a clue or any inside knowledge about visions or plans and goals that you've sketched out for yourself. However, they insist on giving you their views about each of these things. Their opinions of your project may come as scrutiny of your well thought out plans, or negative criticism of each step you make along your journey. Or it could be an elaborate inquiry of you and your project, with no apparent reason for such an interrogation: a barrage of questions that lead to nowhere, which leave you feeling a bit disheartened and disenchanted with things you were once confident about.

 Don't let these people fool you! If they haven't completed a course of life that you admire to the point of mirroring, then don't take any of their advice! Do, however, take advice given from them with a grain of salt.

Perhaps you've had a vision to start a business. Let's say for example that you came across a product that was virtually guaranteed to be profitable within the boating industry. You've done all your homework and you've worked the figures to the best of your ability. You've taken all the necessary steps to become successful in your new venture. Not only have you taken an 8 week course to find out additional information about the business, but you've also consulted with others in the field. Your game is tight, you're ready. But, wait! Here comes an 'expert.' This person has no formal training on the matter that you are about to be involved in. They don't know the first thing about business, and better yet, they probably hate the water and don't even own a boat.

Sound farfetched? Not at all; I've experienced this many times in my past. Therefore, I've given these people the label of 'experts'. They talk as if they know all and can see the outcome of your project, which in their eyes is usually a bad one. It's overtly obvious that these people don't know the first thing about your undertaking.

Since when though, does that stop them from interjecting their thoughts? It doesn't.

'Experts' like to tell you what you should or shouldn't do, and why. They convey to you any and all of the negative possibilities that surround your endeavors. Sometimes they tell you what could've been done better, even after you've successfully completed your project. They like to express what they would've done if they were in your shoes. As a matter of fact, some of them will even start off by stating, "If I was in your shoes…" Another great line is, "You know what you should've done is…" Don't let these 'experts' fool you! Usually, these people are the farthest thing from an expert, as you can get.

Not surprisingly, 'experts' are family, friends, coworkers, or schoolmates. And, although frequently they have good intentions, the energy they confer isn't a productive one. The unfounded thoughts and speculative analysis that they give you might possibly have a damaging effect. Sadly, it could cause you to lose confidence in your capabilities.

Undoubtedly, the reasons they give for handing out such critical judgments on you or your enterprise will be: they are looking out for your best interest, they don't want to see you get hurt or because they love you. Those are all valid reasons; however, some people unknowingly impart their opinions when they themselves are too afraid to take the steps to do or become more, within their own circumstances. Somehow the next best thing to do, in their mind, is to shoot anyone else's idea down (for fear their friend or family member might tread too far away from shore). In other words, they may not have the courage, ambition, and persistence to pursue a lifelong goal which they've desired. In the process, anyone in their circle who *does* is mentally or verbally abused for doing so.

Recognize any 'experts' in your circle of close friends and associates. Realize that their concerns are genuine, but perhaps unsubstantiated. Assure them that this is what you want to do and regardless of the result, it must at least be attempted. Explain that this is a part of your growth as a person and that your life would not be complete without taking a chance to look around the corner to search for new and exciting opportunities. Opportunities may come with some risks, but risks that you've calculated in advance for the best possible outcomes. If the 'expert' feels that he or she *still* knows what's better for you, by continually attempting to dampen your spirit with baseless fears, then go grab the pepper! It would be a nice compliment to those grains of salt.

Ungrateful

There's no joy in scraping the bottom of the barrel
There's no glory in wallowing in pity for yourself
Throwing a party in which no one wants to enter the room
You've left no room for your potential to swell
It's swell that you recognize the void in your life
But what are your plans to correct it?

Do you aspire to rise as cream does?
Or do you choose to stay salty like broth?
Your intentions are good, but you've taken a back seat to
responsibility
Your desire to ride the A train will pass, because you have yet to
climb the stairs

And although seasons change and time passes
You are content, you are settled
just as sediment in the bottom of a five gallon pail
A bucket filled with your dreams and desires
Soon to be washed away, because they've never been used

Is that a silver lining on your cloud?
Or is just some cheap foil to be tossed after one use?
What are your plans for tomorrow, do they consist of the same
nothing you did today?

You've never given yourself a chance to strive
Have you ever felt what it's like to truly be alive
And bask in the glory of all the talent God's given you?

Raecine Tyes

Let's Dream Together

Let's dream together
Cook up a powerful scheme together
Something positive
To showcase our realness
I'm really feelin' this
I think we can be great together
Matter of fact I'm convinced

Your confidence is contagious
Let's support each other
Our success will come in stages
We've left nothing to be desired
We keep rising higher

We've planted seeds together
Let's plot, plan and read together
Inspiration will be endless
Our ideas will attract positive energy
So we'll never be friendless
With our contacts we'll create a powerful synergy

From our dream we'll create a vision
Each other, we'll keep uplifting
Onlookers will be awestruck
Because what we've built has nothing to do with luck

We'll only embrace the good
We'll surround ourselves with positive
Because only then will we really live

This is all something I've seen
When we create our reality from our dream

Disappointments are Steps on the Ladder to Success

Just about everyone gets discouraged about one thing or another, at some point in time. It's so easy to get discouraged too, with all the negative factors surrounding you on a daily basis. People seemingly are always more than happy to tell another individual what they think is or is not possible and their unscientific reasons why. Although you may not be able to control outside circumstances, you can control how you handle yourself, your thoughts and your emotions. Do not allow yourself to become disheartened. And if at all possible, avoid negative influences, and negative people.

Negative emotions have a spiraling effect and if not bridled, can eventually make a bad situation seem even worse than what it actually is. This is one of the instances when it is extremely important to surround yourself with positive people. The support system you have in place will greatly affect how you handle disappointments. With the help of a team biased toward your benefit, you will feel strengthened and empowered to overcome anything!

Of course, there will be times when things don't always go your way, regardless of the support you receive or the amount of time and effort you pour into a project. You must understand that life doesn't stop because of disappointments you personally encounter. So, the best thing to do is realize that if things didn't work the way you hoped for, immediately seek ways to improve the next time.

Whether your disappointment involves a setback in your career, an end to a relationship or a financial misfortune, everything as you may know, is in a constant state of change. Therefore, if something isn't going your way at a particular moment, "Just keep on living," as my grandmother used to say. In other words, nothing is going to stay exactly as it is; these are encouraging words when you know that your situation could use improvement.

Use every disappointment as a stepping stone to make you better, stronger, more resilient and determined toward your success!

Raecine Tyes

Be Determined!

When I think of determination, I think of a person being stubborn, in a very good way. When you are determined, you won't allow anything to stop you or the mission you're on. Too many times, as I've mentioned previously, people let trivial matters stop them from attaining what they set out to do. If I don't stress anything else, it is that you MUST be determined to do whatever it is that you have your heart and mind set on. It is not enough to just have a great idea pop into your mind, casually pursue it until an obstacle appears and then stop when things get a little tough. A determined person would glance over any obstacles with a look of superiority as if to say, "Humpf, you're nothing, I'll get passed you!"

I've watched so many reality shows where the contestants missed out on thousands of dollars because they simply couldn't get along with one another or refused to abide by simple rules. After I verbally expressed to the television set how stupid the contestants are, I realized one thing. Anyone who gets sidetracked from achieving such a large reward in a relatively short period of time just didn't want it bad enough.

When I was pregnant with my second child, I was told to stay on bed rest in my seventh month. It was mainly due to me working and standing most of the pregnancy as a barber. My doctor was fearful of an early delivery as I experienced with my first child. Unable to sit still, and anxious to establish myself as a promoter of business networking events and open mics, I eagerly produced another. Although I was unable to secure a babysitter for every impromptu meeting, while seven months pregnant, my three year old attended conferences, meetings and even a live radio interview in which surprisingly, she sat quiet and still throughout. This is undoubtedly a feat that she would have difficulty doing today as a preteen. Regardless, nothing was going to stop me, I was determined!

What I have learned though, is that for me, determination is like a muscle that needs to get stronger and stronger. You don't have to teach a person to be determined. We all have varied levels of hunger for success. We are different when it comes to how aggressive we are, or are not, when it comes to being determined.

Imagine a bull in the narrow streets of Spain, chasing all the men that have put themselves in his path. Even though there are other happenings in the area, that bull is determined to catch one the fellows running from him. He's determined to unleash his wrath on at least one of the men, and he won't stop until he does so. That's how you and I have to be when it comes to accomplishing our goals and making our visions a reality. Don't stop until you've captured all of your goals and have made the best of them!

Masterminds of Our Vision

I thought we were dreaming together
I thought we'd rise to the top like cream together
Instead, you let all the negativity go to your head

Instead of letting your head swell with thoughts of wealth
You've embraced the weak mind of poverty
Positive thinking is not a novelty

You know all the obstacles we've already faced
Embrace what we still have
Maybe all the voids in our plan can be replaced

Let me lace you with confidence
You're the realest on my team
How can you start slippin?

I'm not feelin all your negative emotions

Why have you kept them bottled up inside?
Why did you hide
what you were feeling?

Maybe if you expressed yourself and atleast made mention
Of the overwhelming stress and tension
that you were experiencing

Either me or another member on our team could encourage you

Empowerment at its upmost,
Because what is most important
is that you keep striving to reach your full potential

Mathematically, we should made it to the top by now
The only thing slowing us down
is the negative influences

Telling us what we can and cannot do

Success Looks Good on Me

Well I refuse to lose based on unscientific opinions
Seeds of discouragement which have no relevance
Placed by provincial gardeners who have yet to reap their harvest

Maybe it's my fault
I had you dreaming

Let's open our eyes wide and create a vision
Cook up a plan, within our minds eye
our souls kitchen

Erase all thoughts of doubt, let go of weak thinking
It's time to become the masterminds of our vision

Create a Vision

If you haven't created a vision for yourself, what are you waiting for? Take a moment to consider these examples: successful construction of any building requires good blueprints, a surgeon doesn't blindly cut into a patient without first considering what has to be done and even a chef gathers all the ingredients he needs to cook a great tasting meal, albeit from a recipe. So, why shouldn't you create a vision for yourself, a plan for your life that includes goals and the steps needed to accomplish them?

For me, creating a clear vision for myself was difficult. I had too many conflicting ideas of what I wanted to do; therefore, it was almost as if I was traveling in circles to get somewhere, and with no end point in sight. Not fun! That is the equivalent to jumping on the highway with no real destination but expecting to end up in a fabulous location for a terrific vacation. Ridiculous! If you have a specific place in mind to go, and you're not exactly sure how to get there, the most logical thing to do would be to either get a road map and map out your journey or put the end address in a GPS device and have it guide you along the way. Either way, you are not traveling blindly to an unspecified end point.

How do you get started with your blueprint, recipe or roadmap to success? It is as simple as picking up a pencil and paper and jotting down ideas that come to mind. Don't restrict your thoughts, just jot down anything that comes to mind no matter how unattainable or farfetched it may seem to be. Initially, if you don't have a vision for yourself or a plan for success, your first step is to create one. Therefore, a pencil and paper are the perfect companions for brainstorming ideas, comparing pros and cons or simply stating your intentions.

 Where do you see yourself in the future? What goals would you like to set for yourself? What actions will you have to take to make those goals come to fruition? What type of time limit do you give yourself to complete your goals and reach your vision? These are only some of the questions to get you started on the pathway to accomplishing more and attaining your goals. However, once you have a clear cut vision, there are definite qualities that you must have to make it a reality. Focus, determination, persistence, flexibility are some of them. Use these qualities to hone your skills and stay motivated to create and realize all of your visions.

I'm so Focused!

When you focus, you have the ability to concentrate on whatever it is that you are doing without letting your surroundings distract you. This is important when you are intent on accomplishing a goal or need to complete a project. If you are focused, mundane or whimsical subject matter will not hinder you or slow you down simply because: you refuse to give attention to it. No doubt you are constantly bombarded everyday with scenarios and situations that could take your time, money or attention away from more important goals or projects you are trying to achieve. You have to make a conscious decision to not let trivial happenings engulf you and take you away from your pursuit of success.

Whether your aspiration entails having the perfect family life, a great career, saving a certain amount of money or being a great sports player, you have to determine what's most important to you and focus on that one thing alone.

 Of course, staying level headed and balanced is best and makes for a well rounded person. However, when it comes down to getting what you want, you have to eat, sleep and dream your own vision; no one else is going to do it for you. You alone know what you want and you alone are the person to make it happen. Getting distracted with sideline ventures that do not compliment your big vision are only going to slow you down, and at worst, completely halt any progress you are making.

How do I know? Well, once again, I'm speaking from experience. When I undertook the project of writing this book, I knew from past experiences and just knowing my own patterns that I would have to stay focused and not allow anything to sidetrack me from what my intentions were. Every day, if I wasn't writing, I'd be thinking about what I was going to write. I'd think of topics to address and how I could attack them with a new, fresh perspective.

 The thought of being an author and completing this book was a mainstay in my mind; otherwise other devices could have easily taken over my thoughts. Tons of other ideas and perpetual projects that I could ensue always crossed my mind, but if I was going to make this book a reality, I had to get a reign on my thinking and stay focused!

Focus is the cousin to determination, because each ensures that you have staying power and are on point. I often reminded myself of how good I'll feel knowing that I completed a specific project and the joy that accompanies it. In addition, I set time limits for myself by writing little notes on the calendar to encourage myself to have specific goals completed by certain dates. This gives any project a sense of urgency so that you can block out non-productive matters. What are some things you do to stay focused?

Second Chances

Money can't buy them
a friend can't give them to you
And even if you get one, it can't erase the first
or erase your thirst
for what should have taken place from the start

A chance to shine
but you only glimmered
a chance to show how hot you are
instead you simmered

A second chance is worth more than gold
More precious than stories untold

A new beginning
where interest may have dwindled
chances to rekindle
what was lost

Second chances should be cherished
They hardly come around
Rarely are they found

To have a second chance is an exceptional opportunity
Use it to the best of your ability
So take it

and accept it

as a blessing

My Biggest Fears

One of my biggest fears
is the world will know that for years,
I was on the Section 8 waiting list

And another fear, which brings me to tears
Is will I make it to heaven, or get lost in the clouds?
And simply disappear

Or maybe after getting invited by Oprah I won't know what to wear

And after careful consideration, I've come to the realization
That I am NOT a supermodel
And never will be

And as for all the possessions I own, am I being grateful enough?
Or when I discipline my children am I too sensitive or too tough?

I'm afraid I won't complete every book that I've bought
And if asked a difficult question, I won't be as smart as you thought

Will you like me or not, after initially meeting me?
Have I shown sufficient generosity, to those in need of me?

If given the chance to choose
Only between the two,
Should I take heart to be more loving
Or courage to face my fears?

Because everything deemed apparent
Is not exactly as it appears

Raecine Tyes

Have Confidence

Just as new, nicely fitted clothes look great on any individual, so does confidence. Confidence has the power to make you feel better about yourself and it also gains others trust in you and in your abilities. When you clothe yourself in confidence great things began to happen. Opportunities open up in your life, people believe in you as a person, and that you can achieve results.

An example of how *not* having enough confidence can slow you down can be noticed by looking at me! I had the idea to write this book many times over, as well as thoughts of becoming a motivational speaker. Time and circumstance didn't stop me, financial obligations didn't slow me down, and other people had no voice in my career decision.

The one and only reason I didn't start my journey to living the vision I had for myself sooner is because I had to build up the confidence in myself. I had to tell myself that my story was worthy of sharing and that I could master whatever project that I wanted to accomplish. I could not allow myself to get caught up in what I thought would or would not work. I could not think about the financial aspect of what I did not have. Instead, I began to focus on projects I successfully completed and other accomplishments in my life. Not only did that boost my self confidence, it also gave me a good feeling to know that I could potentially help another person learn from me.

Think of your past accomplishments and realize how good it made you feel to attain them. Remember, being shy isn't cute if you have great ideas but nobody knows it. Don't suffer silently or settle for less than you are worth solely because you are fearful to voice your opinion on a matter. Show the world what you are made of! *Step out on faith, believe in yourself, erase all doubts and live your dreams!* Perhaps you will influence another person to greatness; at that point, not only are you confident, you are influential too!

Anyone who truly knows me knows that I've done some major transformations in my lifetime and becoming organized is one of them. I'm not sure if it was a phase I went I through, or if I just got tired of not being able to find anything but I'm no longer the 'messy freak' I once was.

Now, I'm a border line 'neat freak'. As a teenager, I can remember having piles of clothes in my bedroom completely covering the whole floor, drawers with any and everything thrown in them, and a closet that could probably transport Dorothy to anyplace she desperately desired to go, even home.

Let's not get it twisted though, I was never the type to leave sandwiches in bags and forget about them. That was something I reserved for my sister, and trust me; a month old peanut butter and jelly sandwich is not appealing!

As a 19 year old newlywed, I hated when unannounced visitors stopped by. It was understandable that I only wanted to be bothered with my new husband; however, that was not the main reason for my aggravation. Before anyone stepped foot in our condo, we'd run around like crazy people throwing dirty dishes in the dishwasher, grabbing dirty clothes and tossing them into an already packed closet. We'd do whatever else it took to make it look like we were normal, clean human beings.

I'll never forget my first child, my eleven pound bichon frise, Babet Snow. Named by her previous owner, Be Be would often happily get lost in piles of dirty laundry that my first husband and I would allow to accumulate in our bedroom. Pathetic!

Looking back at how I once lived, I must've been crazy. There's nothing attractive about living in a messy environment. To me there is a definite difference between being messy and being dirty. Either one is bad, but I was always more of the messy type versus the nasty, dirty type.

I have friends that won't set foot into a car if it looks dirty and my children too, immediately notice homes that are dirty and like me, are reluctant to eat or make use of the facilities in such a place.

Disorganization encourages disunity, within your own mind and with others who share your dwelling. Whether it is at work or home, a clean, clutter free space is relaxing and comforting. It is also an environment that is conducive to creativity. Take time to organize your surroundings. Clutter and mess can be a major distraction and hinder you from becoming the person you know you are capable of being. Your brain will thank you.

It Aint Enough

It's not enough that your momma work almost every day of the week
to provide a place to stay, and something to eat
She'll spend her last on your- Ask her how she's doing sometime
And even though, she might say fine, she don't mean it
She's just saving face and showing grace,
Because...that's what a lady does

And its not enough that your family barely got enough food to last
till the end of the week
What you go and do with your little bit a money, you spent it on
something that look good on your feet...that don't make no sense!

And you think you'd have enough, cause you had one baby, but you
had to go back and get two or more,
Yeah, they cute, they're something to adore
But do you have enough food for that baby to eat
Can you provide that baby with a warm clean place to sleep
Did that baby's father pass ninth grade, can he read?
Does he even want to be bothered with his own seed??

Y'all don't hear me!

And why you go and pull that weave out that girls head?
Over something your man supposedly did, and something she
supposedly said?
That ain't cute!

And I know y'all had enough of the Feds all up and down the Ave
They trying to make you realize the difference between what you
actually got
and what you ain't *never* had
Yeah, you may have a piece of the rock, but that sidewalk, that you
claiming as your block,
That ain't yours!

And I know you have had enough of your friend, your neighbor, and
your cousin getting shot!

Raecine Tyes

and *all* they left on this earth, was a corpse to rot!

And it's not enough that we got a black president up in office
Even though he told us...*Yes we can!*

Cause your still doing the same malarky," It's not me!" is the first
thing that you say
Well, I'm the realist poet, and I'm telling you what's on my mind
today

I'm the realist poet that you ever gonna meet, but you still think I'm
playin games

Well, I wish I knew each and every one of your first and last names,
because

I'd take you to school and tell you when class is outta session
To have someone up in your face, who cares, now that's a blessing!

Don't feel like you're stuck in your situation, just know what to do
You're expected to
Set a goal or two
Take some chances, make some advances
And create for your life
Your own, cir-cum-STANCES!!!

Be Limitless

Recently, I was talking with a friend who shot down every idea I had about a project he was working on. He felt that he didn't have the proper equipment he needed and that it was going to be impossible to obtain it. Every time I mentioned what he would need to do or have to purchase, he'd tell me why or how he wouldn't be able to. I jokingly told that person that I was going to have to get a chisel to open up his mind to all the possibilities around him. In response he asked, "Do my ideas seem as if I'm thinking limited?"

I answered him, "No, you don't have limited thinking, but you are limiting *yourself* when you think that you don't have enough resources, money or equipment. You *will* and *can* have those things. You just don't have them right now." And then I reminded him of the old saying, "Where there is a will, there is a way." He seemed to forget that old saying, or at least he wasn't putting faith in those words. Most times, when impossible situations arise, it's easy to see only see what is smack in front of your face. You may be so focused in on your obstacle that you don't see all the solutions surrounding you. Sometimes answers to dilemmas seemingly come out of nowhere. I can attest to that.

New projects too, can appear overwhelming if you think about all that needs to be accomplished. Don't limit yourself by dwelling on what you don't have, can't do or don't know. *Realize now that there is a solution to every problem* and that's what you have to zoom in on, your solutions. If you stop in your tracks because of a few difficulties, then ultimately you are limiting yourself to any opportunities along your life journey.

Whether you are seeking solutions to a problem, new business ideas, a topic for a research paper or a theme for your next party, don't limit yourself. Innovative inventions, jaw dropping entertainment, and creative service businesses wouldn't have a chance without one single person who wasn't afraid to let his or her mind soar with possibilities. Spunky ice cream flavors, breathtaking architectural designs, and even funky baby names are expressions of a limitless mind. Don't cheat yourself from experiencing life at its fullest! Focus on your desired results, and then allow your mind to wander without restraint. Filter out needless thoughts afterward. In the meantime be creative, be imaginative and be limitless!

Set Standards for Yourself

If there is one thing I've learned over the years, it's that you have to set a standard for your life and stick with it. Refuse to settle for less than you deserve! The only person that knows your hearts true desires, wants, fears, inadequacies and motives is you! So, rather than give in to a scenario or situation that is not in accord with your life path, pause, and make necessary realignments. Many times people have allowed circumstances to occur in their life that they were unhappy about. Afterwards, they act bewildered as to how they ended up with such a scenario.

You must understand that whether it is a moral, physical, romantic, financial or personal situation, *anything that has taken place in your life is because you allowed it.* For many people, this is a hard pill to swallow because it is so much easier to claim yourself as a victim and accept pity from others. In this way, if a certain level of success isn't achieved, they have someone else to blame.

I had to recognize and apply this very principle of accepting only what is best for me and nothing less. By mentally setting standards of what I would and would not allow or what I would or would not *do* in my life, regrets would be near nil. Everything that happened to me is something I'd given thought to and took full responsibility for, whether the outcome was good or bad, I'd accepted them in advance. Therefore, when the results to any situation are unfavorable, I can truthfully say to myself, "I have no one to blame, but me." Not only will this cut down on tension, strife and heartache with others, but you will know that you've done the best that you can to make yourself as happy as possible.

Also, never be content with just getting by, no matter what the case may be. Just as my grandmother used to say, "Whatever you are doing, no matter what it is, be the best at it." Set high standards for yourself and strive to reach them. Your efforts won't go unnoticed. Realize too, that you are worthy of the best. Don't settle for what you don't like or want. In the end, when you set high standards, everybody benefits.

Raecine Tyes

My Silence

My silence is often louder than the hustling and bustling of people
headed off to work

And what works for me is if I play a little game and try not to blame
myself for things in my life that didn't work

It's quite simple you see, I don't claim responsibility, for failures,
although they're mine

And sometimes when I think I'm losing my mind, somehow it
always finds its way back to me

And it's always in the nick of time

FaceBook Fanatic

FaceBook fanatic!
Another day and you're back at it
Spend a minute or two reminiscing, now you're tripping
On friends you thought you'd lost, never to see again
At what cost, would you pay to rewind
And go back in time?

Once again, they're back in your life
"Nice" doesn't begin to describe
The way you feel inside,
When a profile of an old friend you've recognized
It's hard to imagine all the years gone by
A few tears, may come to your eye
Who thought seeing an old friend would have such an impact?

Now you're sending hugs and blowing kisses
Accept, confirm, now you're enlisted
Into a network of friends, colleagues and ex- schoolmates
Who now have mates, and families of their own
Some whose kids are full grown

Change your status to reflect your day
Or review what others have to say
About a question posed, or a subject on your wall
Although it's impossible to please all
LOL lightens the mood, even when the response is rude

Notes and photos in which you were tagged
They make you laugh. "Dag!"
The eighties were crazy!
Styles back then were a definite maybe

FaceBook gives you a chance to update and upgrade,
Share with the world the changes you've made
Tiny red notifications, event invitations

Chat with friends and reveal old crushes

Raecine Tyes

Pass a drink is creating virtual lushes

Shameless self promotion like Raecine is doing
New connections too and a few romances brewing
FaceBook members really spread the love
Although I'm still trying to figure out…"What's a booty hug"?

The Associates

Let me share with you a story of inspiration
It's the day I came to my realization
It's about some of my "associates" from way back when
I wouldn't call them my friends
Because I don't want to be known by them
I hadn't seen them in a while
But it was for the best
Because they were cramping my style

You see, I have no time to waste
It's time to pick up my pace
First *Opposition* stepped to me
I told him to get out of my face

Next, I told *Anxiety*
Not to even say hi to me
And I ignored *Disillusioned*,
So he wouldn't have a chance to come cry to me

Fear was too scared, so he sent his rep in
But once I found out, I told him to get to steppin'
Miss *Shy* walked by, trying to be cute
"Pfffffftt"- I gave her the boot!

I peeked out my window and saw *Procrastination* waiting
But he was hating
Because I was chillin' with *Forethought*
So I wasn't even hesitating

Disbelief came in with her companion, *Doubt*
But I told her, "Look baby, up in here you don't have no clout"
Because if I didn't believe it, I wouldn't have seen it
And without the desire, I wouldn't have even dreamed it
So I deemed it necessary even vital
To never give up and never sit idle

Right about that time, *Content* sashayed by trying to relax me

Raecine Tyes

But here's the good part
That's when *Reality* smacked me

Ambition picked me up and shook off my dust
Cause it's a must, to keep it moving
If I'm going to accomplish my goals
I'm on a roll
That's when *Persistence* helped me out
Some think he's rude
But he's a good dude

He introduced me to *Focus* (he only got one eye)
So he's not ever concerned with other things going by
I can't wait to meet *Wisdom*, but that'll come in time
They say after getting with him, he always on your mind

I've learned new lessons almost everyday
And I can still hear those four words Grand Mama used to say
"Just keep on livin" meaning you gonna see more,
So don't be surprised
Just keep your eyes open wide
And don't miss a step in your stride

Cause when you miss a beat
Those bad associates attack you
But if you got a plan
Confidence will back you

There's a difference between searching and looking
Maybe one day you'll find
That all the answers you'll ever need are in your own mind

And the chances of you reaching your goals
Are much more than probable
And with some new associates, I mean friends…
You'll become unstoppable!

Looking Back

People are obsessed with looking back. People like to reminisce about things that happen years earlier and remember how things used to be. Old pictures have the ability to start long conversations about past events and situations that were long forgotten. Memories conjure up feelings strong enough to propel a person into action. Retro items never go out of style and can be found at just about any market place you go into. Friends that you haven't seen or talked to in years are greeted and embraced as if they'd never missed a day together. Looking back to experiences in the past can be fun but also eye opening. The expression "Hind sight is 20/20" is so true! Individuals act and react to situations in the present, because of experiences they had in the past.

However, *if you want to be successful at anything in your life, it is always better to keep focused on your future.* Many times, an individual may express what he or she desires to happen in the future, yet they constantly look to past experiences and wallow in disappointing ventures. I've heard it said that your future is a book waiting to be written, and your past is a movie that has already been played. Whether you treasure the events in the past or have regrets, it's all said and done. There is nothing that can be done to change your experience. There are no time machines, no magical potions or any type of therapy that can alter the past.

The only thing that you are capable of is to ensure that your future is as best as it can be. If you want to duplicate great results that you experienced in the past, that's great! But what improvements can you make? If there are circumstances you found yourself in that were harmful or hurtful, take steps to ensure that it won't happen again because you've had an example from the past. Make sure you put whatever has happened to you in the past in the proper context and use it as a learning lesson, whether good or bad. Never let anything in your past slow you down or stop you from reaching your goals. Resolve now to let your past spur you on to greatness in the future!

Easy Come, Easy Go

As much nonsense that I've been through, survived and triumphed, I now realize that no matter what happens to me that there is no need to get discouraged. If you receive a major blow to your finances, career or relationship, don't let yourself wallow in it, rather empower yourself and be determined to master your emotions, because they control your whole outlook on life and your psyche.

I learned long time ago when I was a senior in high school that material things can go just as easily as you get them. One such example is my class ring that I saved so diligently for, a 14K gold ring which I chose a diamond as the center stone, on a 14K gold nugget setting. For this extra bit of extravagance, I paid a hefty sum more than my classmates who got the usual hum drum birthstones and settings. Weeks after ordering it, I anxiously anticipated its arrival; and when I finally had it in my possession, I cherished it. However, that was short lived.

That summer, I frequented the beach as I usually did, but this time I was accompanied by my new beau, who would eventually become my first husband. While exchanging frivolous pleasantries at the beach, my ring landed on his finger which eventually ended up, in the sand; that was the end of that. Even though a group of us searched as thoroughly as we possibly could, my ring was gone...forever. Surprisingly, I wasn't as upset as I thought I'd be in a situation like that; as a senior in high school, I paid a *relatively* large sum of money for that ring. However, it was my choice to purchase it, and my decision to allow another person to wear it, so I had no one to blame, but myself. I was a little disheartened, but I couldn't allow myself to get mad or discouraged. After all, it was a material item and at least all my friends and family had a safe, fun time at the beach and everyone left just as healthy as they came.

Other such occasions in which my material items became a memory instantly are when I lost personal items and expensive clothing along with priceless schoolwork and memoirs from when I was a child because of careless decision. It was hard to swallow at first, but it was a costly lesson that I had to learn, a lesson that would stay with me forever. Now I categorize situations in my life and give them proper priority, so that I'll no longer be faced with dilemmas such as that again.

Hurricanes, tornadoes, fires and other acts of God can just as easily wipe out any and everything a person owns. Unfortunately the United States has seen one of the worst instances of this with Hurricane Katrina. Regretfully, I have had automobiles too, that have come and gone, either from being repossessed or wrecked. If you are determined to have nice things and you are persistent in your pursuit of wealth, you will acquire the things that you desire to have. However, it is always a good reminder that such possessions can disappear, just as easily as they came.

Real Talk

Real talk
I like you a lot

Your mannerisms
Your personality
I even love the way you walk

And the color of your skin
Has nothing to do with it
I'm even cool if
it's not the same color as mine
I'd be a fool if I thought you weren't fine

I refuse to put superficial preconditions on who could potentially be
my soul mate,
Racial prejudice is something that I hate
I can't relate

To those people that subscribe to the philosophy, that the color of
skin
is more important than what can be found deep within

Because your heart is what truly matters
And the heart of the matter is

You are delicious

No matter what flavor you come in
Whether it's brown, yellow, black, pearly white or cinnamon

As a matter of fact,
I'm ecstatic that

You chose me as your significant other
And when you tell me all the reasons why,
none of them is my color

Success Looks Good on Me

Don't get me wrong, I love how your skin glows in the moonlight
And when the sun hits you just right

Your eyes smile
It's been a while

Since I felt this way about someone

You got me talkin' about moonlight, and how you look in the sun

More importantly is how you make me feel inside
I'm letting my conscious be my guide
So far everything is going just right

I've tallied my votes and the results are in
This thing we got, has nothing to do
with the color of our skin

Beautifully, They Love

A love story for the ages
One written down on history pages

Involving more than romantic notions
And love potions

This story has many mystified
Even teary eyed
at the prospect of what can be.

Hope given to all, in awe
People of all races they've drawn

They encompass not only love, but intellect
Their daughters, they never neglect
From millions, they've gained respect

Though publicly they serve
Undoubtedly, quiet moments they cherish
Through public displays of affection,
they are not embarrassed.

With a glance, a whisper or a bump of the fists
Even a quick kiss,
How can one miss, the love they share?

Subtlety, they prove
as a man and woman
they are not only father and mother
but lovers.

Powerfully, they command attention.

Wonderfully, they inspire.

Beautifully, they love.

It's no longer 'me,' now it's 'us'
and that's just
the way I like it

What's so amazing is, I've known you for over a decade
and you've never made
my heart jump like this before

You waited for all foolishness to subside
then you confided in me
and professed your love

We were always only friends
solemente amigos
And now you've asked me to be your partner for life
It feels so right

When you asked for my hand
it was a definite yes
I feel so blessed

knowing that you're my gift from God

Calm Before the Storm

Prosperous like black wealth
Our love is continuously growing,
We're making moves with this music thang
And the growth in our relationship is showing

To have you in my life is a blessing
Together, we can weather any type of storm, no stressing

Your love is a therapy for my soul
I don't mind if you're in my life until we both grow old

With the music we're making
Represent, then stand up-Salute!
We're the truth
For years you've been in my life, and we're still in our youth

So time is on our side
We're making lovely music; it's a part of our life
We're avoiding all the low notes and hitting all the highs

We're seeing results from the gift God's given us
We pray for his guidance, so He keeps uplifting us

We're rising to the top, I hear them calling our names
We're destined for fame

Calm before the storm
But we've been thru the thick of it
You get out what you put in, so we're determined to stick with it
One year and four months our hearts have been sick with it

We're not just music lovers; we're in love with each other

I still get a thrill during the day when you text me
And others are hating because we're "Oh so sexy"

Calm before the storm

Success Looks Good on Me

But we've endured for better weather
Taking advantage of all opportunities
Because we're in this together

Calm before the storm, but we have no worries
Everything in due time, so no need to hurry

We're blessed!
Sharing our love while living out our passion
With no regrets, we're moving on to what's next

Now grab hold of my hand and put your other on the mic
I love the music we make and I love you in my life

Sour Love

Your blank stare speaks to me
but it's telling me words that I don't want to hear
I'm in denial about your feelings for me

I am suspect at the prospect of being alone
and I don't think I can bear to hear those words
that have silently crept past my heart
right down to the pit of my belly
where all things have gone sour

Including your love for me

I'm reaching, i'm trying to grasp on to any inkling
of what we have, my mistake, what we had
is there anything left?

Just as a child scrapes an empty jar of preserves
all of our sweetness is gone
Have we anything to preserve?

Ebonics

I am powerless until on paper I scribble,
From my mouth thoughts dribble.

But do my words cease to have meaning if I speak incorrectly?
Does the manner in which I speak, directly, affect me?

Is my speech so dramatically mangled and dismantled
That you can't get a handle on what I'm saying to you?

Or maybe I'm lazy or just a bit crazy for not eloquently expressing
The thoughts I'm relaying to you

The evolution of my people is now taking place,
A people from which our culture was raped

The evolution of my people is still taking place,
How else do you explain the same mannerisms
Same home cookin' from state to state?

A creation of speech, dress, movement and music,
Does Ebonics enhance or just confuse it?

Surround Yourself with Positive People

It is so important to always surround yourself with positive people! Imagine: You are invited out for the evening, but you aren't exactly sure where you are going. You arrive to a room full of people who don't say one word to you; however their facial expressions give the impression that they are mad. Everyone is walking around the room without acknowledging you, intentionally not speaking to you and they are also giving you harsh looks. Not a very inviting feeling at all...is it? You may begin to wonder, "What have I done?" and afterwards think, "I need to get out of here!"

Or, perhaps you walk in that same room but this time, everyone has a Kleenex in their hand, wiping tears from eyes, hugging and consoling one another. Again, you instantly recognize the mood in the room and you may again want to leave before your good mood begins to dampen. You realize that their negative moods will eventually bring yours down too.

On the other hand, what if you enter a room full of giggling people, who are smiling, patting each other on the back, and they all have checks in each of their hands? Well, you'd probably want to stick around, because in this case you'd welcome the opportunity for each of their good emotions to rub off on you! They probably gave you a good feeling and any bad thoughts you had previous to entering the room may have even disappeared from your mind.

Each situation deals with other people's emotions and their impact on us. So, we know that whatever vibe we are around is going to directly affect us. More importantly, if we are around a negative vibe, after a while we may start to lose our focus on anything productive we have going on. Can you think of a time when you were happy and anxious to go somewhere but your whole demeanor changed because of a phone call or some bad news? Afterwards, you may have even thought to yourself, "I don't even feel like going now!" Well it's the same concept.

Sometimes, negative influences can be subtle. So what can we do to make sure the people we associate with are positive and a good influence in our lives? Here are a few questions I came up with to help you (and me) determine if this is a person you want to spend time with.

1. Does this person support my vision whether they understand it or not?
2. Does this person talk about new ideas rather than always talking about non-productive matters?
3. Do they push me to do more and encourage me to reach my full potential or do they constantly tell me what I can't do and why?
4. Do they encourage me when I'm feeling down or are they continually putting me down?
5. Does this person look for the best in other people?
6. Is this person always in a bad mood or do they always have some sort of continuing problem with other people?
7. How do I feel when I'm around this person? Do I feel good when I'm in their presence or do I always leave them feeling down or bad?

Weigh your answers and if they don't add up, limit your time with that individual, *or let them know you are accepting only positive into your life from this point on.* Tell them kindly, that you no longer want to subscribe to any negativity. Unfortunately, it can sometimes be a friend or a relative who is a negative factor; this doesn't mean you don't love them any less! Try to help them see the benefits of being more positive. However, if you stay around any negativity too long, you are only hurting yourself! Stay positive, think positive! Surround yourself with positive people!

Stay Motivated

Staying motivated is the number one dilemma people face while striving to attain goals. Words of encouragement from a friend, acknowledgement for previous achievements or a nod of acceptance by a loved one are usually enough to give a boost towards accomplishing even more in your life. Just as a coach pushes an athlete to do his best, even when the athlete doesn't recognize his own potential, most people would excel if they had a similar type of motivator. We could all use a person to give us the best play by play pointers for our life, or insight on important decisions which could ultimately propel us to success at an accelerated rate. However, most people can't afford the luxury of employing such an aggressive support system or personal cheerleaders. Therefore, self motivation is the key, but how?

Because different things motivate different people, you have to identify for yourself what works best for you. A few basic tips that I've come up with to help me include the following:

1. Recognize your talents and remember that these are what make you special.
2. Categorize distractions in relation to priority or totally eliminate and ignore them.
3. Create solutions rather than dwell on problems.
4. Make a list of goals and take action steps, no matter how small, towards accomplishing them.
5. Focus on the positive in any situation to attract positive energy.
6. Surround yourself with positive people, negative people will drain you.
7. Master your emotions! Emotions determine your state of mind; pick yourself up when feeling down.

Make it Happen!

You've read different success techniques. You've created a vision for yourself and put a list of goals down on paper. You've told other people about the plans you have for a special project or expressed to a confidant accomplishments you want to make, or aspirations you have. What do you do next? Make it happen! "Don't talk about it, be about it," I'm sure you've heard that one liner before. Now it's *your* turn to "be about it." Everything looks good down on paper, now it's time to make your words come alive.

You've pictured yourself in your vision being successful. Are you seeking a better position at your job or perhaps a more fulfilling career? Do you desire to shed the roommate and find a place of your own? Are you determined to become a more generous person? Don't you think your weight loss goals deserve some attention? Don't keep talking about what you are going to do, and how great things will be after the fact. Get started being the person that you desire to be, today!

Anyone can make a list of goals, desires and wishes. *But how many people actually follow thru and accomplish what they set out to do?* Keep in mind that you don't have to do things in leaps and bounds, nobody is a Superman. Do what you can to make your plans a reality. If your long term project requires you to receive special training, then at least check out the schools in your local area. Visit a few schools or call to find out what classes are required to be successful in your new career.

Use different success techniques to help you achieve your vision. Remember that procrastination stalls progress, so don't wait too long before you attack your goals. Stay positive and focused on what you want, regardless of any obstacles that come your way. Surround yourself with positive people that will support you and give you constructive feedback. Optimize all of your resources and network with individuals who can help you on your quest.

Remember that success is all about having a good plan and never giving up on it. Resolve to make your visions reality! Accomplish all that you set out to do! Once you've traveled your journey and paid your dues, you'll realize that success is right around the corner, waiting for you!

Tell Somebody, To Tell Somebody

Have you ever told somebody a juicy tidbit of information, in confidence, and realized only a few days later that it spread like wild fire? It happened because your friend told his friend, who passed the information on to a few other friends. That process continued until it probably got right back to you. Imagine getting free or discounted services using that same concept of communication.

We each have a circle of friends, family and associates that we communicate with regularly. If you are in the process of completing a project or if you need assistance accomplishing a goal, why not turn to someone in your network? Perhaps they can offer you some guidance; or maybe they can put you in touch with someone who can help you skip a few steps, in your quest to success. The old saying, "It's not what you know, rather it's who you know," always holds weight. Put the word out that you seek certain items or specialized knowledge to reach your goals. Anyone who has a desire to support you will pass that information along to individuals they feel who can help you.

If you don't have a network, get out and mingle! If you are serious about gaining new contacts, attend industry related events, with other people in attendance who have similar interests. Connect with a small group of people who you can trade resources with and continuously branch out. You have to have genuine intentions and uphold your side of the deal though. That's what networking is all about.

Don't expect to prosper via your network and not give back. It's only reasonable that you offer your skills to anyone who has given their time or services to you. I've made a habit of helping others out on events or promotions, to gain experience for future clients and projects of my own. Colleagues are usually grateful that I've dedicated myself to support them in their endeavor and most people are eager to return the favor. I always tell people, "If I help you, I'm helping myself."

Raecine Tyes

Although, remember my chapter about the "experts." Don't get caught up taking foul advice from an individual who doesn't know what they are talking about. Make sure your confidant is a person who understands and supports your vision, and only has your best interests at heart. Having a good network can be a crucial part in you overcoming obstacles and reaching your goals with ease. Make your network work for you.

Once Again

Once again,
You've given me your best
When I'm feeling unsettled
You helped me to rest

Intellectually, You've always taught me
With wisdom and life experiences.
But Spiritually You've brought me

Along on a journey to find
Peace within my weary soul
You've calmed my worried mind.

Once again,
You've held my heart, when I wallow in sorrow.
And with comforting thoughts
You've told me to look to tomorrow.

You've placed people in my life,
Who unknowingly inspire me.
Their words and deeds
Spark a small fire in me

I eagerly accept all that You're teaching me
Although patiently, You've repeated Yourself
So many times!

I think it's finally reaching me.

I worked out a plan
Then Your purpose came into play
Once again, because of Your love
I bend my knees and humbly say,

"Thank you!"

A. S. A. P.

You can read as many self help, motivational and inspirational books as you want. You can participate in expensive seminars, attend workshops and listen to audio recordings. However, if you sit on the information and don't take any action, you may as well sit on a goose egg because you'll get the absolute same results with both: *nothing*. Although, when you do take the first step on your journey to success, you should do it as speedily as possible. This is done for a few reasons.

First, you don't want to lose any momentum you've built up to help you succeed in your new project. When you brainstorm after returning home from a special event, ideas pop in your head from out of nowhere. Don't take that time for granted! Collect ideas when they are fresh; they'll give you a bright and original perspective on your new venture.

Second, the faster you take action, the less likely you will let negative thinking and influences seep into your plans. The quicker you begin striving for your goal, the sooner you will see results from your efforts. Finally, you don't want to give procrastination a chance to settle in. Procrastination can be dissolved with immediate action.

Imagine two people walking down a busy city street. One is walking at a relaxed pace, continuously glancing down at a map, with a nonchalant attitude; the other person has a little bit of speed, with a look of determination and is focused on his end point. Which person do you think will reach their destination and seemingly overcome obstacles with ease? Who do you think nobody will mess with, because he looks "all about his business"?

I'm not saying to rush and tend to your tasks haphazardly, or to get started without proper tools. Get what you need to accomplish your goals and be prepared to overcome dilemmas, however, don't waste time doing it. Get everything done in a timely manner so you can reach your goals as soon as possible. Once you get moving, keep it moving!

Uplift With It

I'm incurable
I'm sick with it

I sit, fiddle and pick with it
But since I've gotten better
I'm thinking, I'll stick with it

Maybe one day I'll get rich from it
I'll find my own niche with it

If my pen was a camera I'd take a flick with it
But instead I'm thanking Bic for it

I have my own style
I'm chic with it

Sometimes I have you rotfl
I'll put you in a fit with it

My writing is taking me places
I'm a trip with it

Sometimes I think, dream, ponder
And just sit with it

I'm blessed to have this talent
So others I try to uplift with it

Time stops for no one
That's why I'm swift with it

My presence to enjoy another day on this earth is golden
But God's hand in my life is a gift with it

Raecine Tyes

Help You to Help Yourself

Of all the things that you can do to be successful in your day to day activities, there is one very important action you can do at night: Sleep! *Never underestimate the power of sleep.* It's not uncommon to get caught up in the everyday hustle and then try to cram everything that has to be done, for that day, well into the night. I know because I'm guilty of that. I can't count how many times I've been up many hours past midnight finishing school projects, perming my hair, watching movies, talking on the phone, reading or writing, and even cooking; my mother calls me a night hawk. Certain individuals are early birds, but some people are at their best at night. That's fine, but what's even better is if you have a scheduled time to relax, unwind and go to sleep.

Your body consists of organs which perform particular functions and some do their main jobs at night. If you don't give your body sufficient rest on a continuous basis, not only will you look crazy, but it will take a toll on your health and your system won't work properly. Some of my friends prefer the term rest to sleep. Whatever you call it, just do it!

Previously, I've stressed the importance of being focused, determined, and confident among other qualities to achieve your personal best. It was just the other day I overheard my bank teller saying to her coworker, "I'm so tired, I don't know what to do." I've said that myself, a thousand times, when I didn't get the proper amount of rest the night before. Tell me, how are you going to be focused on a new venture if all you can think about is catching a few winks? Determined? The *only thing* you'll be determined to do is to close your eyes, as soon as you can. And confident; I don't think you'll look too confident slouched over, leaning on everyone and everything, just to keep yourself up. I think you get the point.

If you are one of those people that have a difficult time resting during the night, there are certain things you can do to calm and relax yourself. A warm bath, a soothing body massage, soft music, a good book or a hot cup of decaffeinated tea can all help you to unwind and prepare for bedtime. Be sure to limit your caffeine intake during the day too, so you won't have the urge to run a marathon when your day is ending. If possible try to steer clear of chemical dependants to encourage sleep.

There are dangers in oversleeping as well as the harm, to be had, in not getting enough rest. Do what you must to make sure you have a balanced amount of sleep for your age and circumstances. There's nothing better than to get a bright eyed, fresh start on your goals each morning. After all, the early bird gets the worm! You do want some worms, don't you?

Positively Thinking

So, you've read a motivational book, took notes, signed up for a class and you even walked around the block a few times to finally get started on your new exercise regime; somehow you don't feel it's enough and you don't see any results. As my husband says, "Slow down tiger!" At least you've made the first steps and that is the most important thing to do.

Don't get caught up with the mindset that television commercials would like you to have, in which you need everything now, fast and immediately. This is the real world; we can't Photoshop our blemishes, erase obstacles or fast forward to the next scene. I've learned to take each day as it comes and do everything that I can to make that particular day a success within itself.

If you are working toward a lifelong goal, don't be discouraged due to the long time frame you may need to see results; rather be happy knowing each day that you did a little something to reach your full potential. If you've started a new regimen to lose weight, be content with the fact that until you reach your goal weight, from this point on, you are healthier than the day before.

Keep a positive frame of mind no matter what your situation is. What's the use in worrying about dilemmas that you can't fix instantly? Focus on the solutions to obstacles and stay fixed on the end results of all your efforts, regardless of how small of and effort it may be. Stay busy with activities that involve your passion. Create opportunities for others who enjoy similar interests. Occupy your mind with what has to be completed before you can reach the next level of your success.

Resolve to accept the outcome of decisions you've made. Be happy with yourself when small accomplishments are realized. Freely praise yourself and others to keep a positive vibe. Read inspirational material and eat healthy so your mind, body and spirit can exude positive energy. Be empowered and become a source of inspiration for others!

Raecine's Message to You

As a single mother I've searched almost everywhere to gain knowledge that would make my existence on this earth, not only easier, but productive. I've read books upon books and listened intently to wise people; I've taken lessons from personal experiences and used my own common sense. I've also prayed for understanding of everything that I've learned.

Somewhere on my journey, I cultivated a passion for empowering individuals with the information I uncovered. I realized too, that by encouraging others, I had to focus on the positive, which was great for me. My circle of support was a relatively small one; therefore, I appreciate any and all sources of inspiration. I urge you to be grateful for what you have. You will be blessed with more. When you are, share your knowledge. Wherever you find encouragement, embrace it.

Work your plan and never give up on it, no matter what obstacles you face. Keep an optimistic outlook and enjoy the company of positive people.

Plant seeds for your success by recognizing opportunities and taking advantage of them. Things may not happen at the exact time that you wish, but the end result could be much more than you imagined, so be patient. Work diligently toward your goals and God will make you flourish.

Sincerely,

Raecine Tyes